Sex,
Literature,
and Censorship

ALSO BY D. H. LAWRENCE

Sex,
Literature,
and Censorship

BY D. H. LAWRENCE

Edited by Harry T. Moore

The Viking Press · New York

VIKING COMPASS EDITION

ISSUED IN 1959 BY THE VIKING PRESS, INC.

625 MADISON AVENUE, NEW YORK, N.Y. 10022

FIFTH PRINTING MAY 1969

DISTRIBUTED IN CANADA BY

THE MACMILLAN COMPANY OF CANADA LIMITED

LIBRARY OF CONGRESS CATALOG CARD NUMBER: 59-65295

P N B

PRINTED IN THE U.S.A. BY THE COLONIAL PRESS INC.

Contents

When Adam went and took Eve, *after* the apple, he didn't do any more than he had done many a time before, in act. But in consciousness he did something very different. So did Eve. Each of them kept an eye on what they were doing, they watched what was happening to them. They wanted to KNOW. And that was the birth of sin. Not *doing* it, but KNOWING about it. Before the apple, they had shut their eyes and their minds had gone dark. Now, they peeped and pried and imagined. They watched themselves. And they felt uncomfortable after. They felt self-conscious. So they said, "The *act* is sin. Let's hide. We've sinned."

  —D. H. LAWRENCE, *Studies in Classic American Literature*

Preface to the Compass Edition

By Harry T. Moore

In the thirtieth year after D. H. Lawrence's death, his name perkily ascended the American best-seller lists, and week after week it stayed high up there as the nation at last read the unexpurgated version of *Lady Chatterley's Lover*. This belated public interest in Lawrence, or at least in one of his books, followed the rise of his reputation in literary circles, where after a period of obscurity he had recently been promoted from a minority writer to an author of magnitude.

During the first excitement over the American publication of *Lady Chatterley*, some intellectuals felt that Lawrence was being read "for the wrong reasons": most of the seasoned investigators of his writings do not consider *Lady Chatterley* to be among his finest work. But surely many of the readers attracted to that novel will become curious about *The Rainbow* and *Women in Love* and other books which the specialists think are among Lawrence's best. Of course much more than this can be said on the favorable side in regard to reading the full text of *Lady Chatterley*. Whatever the artistic limitations of this novel, it remains a significant and influential work by a major writer, and it contains an important statement about the human condition. Above all, it is not a "dirty" book. The essays in the present volume will help readers to understand why all this is true, and why Lawrence is a supremely important prophetic writer.

The writings collected here range widely over the subjects of love, sex, art, and censorship; they are rich with the implications of their themes and marked by a lively variety of tone. In them we can see Lawrence's good sense in abundance and can understand why so many of the "daring" things he said have become part of our heritage and yet remain so fresh. We can also feel the warmth of Lawrence's humor and, just occasionally, the fierce edge of his anger.

He invariably gritted his teeth when he spoke of what he called "the censor-morons," who had plagued him from the beginning of his career. His troubles with various kinds of censorship are well known. Yet, despite these vexations, this man being eaten away by tuberculosis rather amazingly lived halfway into his forty-fifth year, writing vigorously to the last.

Serious readers soon discover that Lawrence was a profoundly moral man and that he was obsessed not with sex but with life. This comes through every line of his writing, through the seething colors, the vibrant portraits, and the cadences of a style that suggests Biblical rhythms blended with the colloquial speech so often found in the main tradition of English literature. This full expression of life is often concerned with love, not mere sex: with love as one of the great oppositions to the mechanization of humanity. Lawrence, growing up in the Nottinghamshire coalfield in the decline of the Victorian age, was conditioned by that era and by the Congregationalism of the miners' bethel of his childhood. In his later reaction away from the Victorian-puritan attitude, he saw how its restrictions and hypocrisies united with the regularizing elements of industrialism to crush out the primary emotions, particularly love. *Lady Chatterley,* which treats love almost sacramentally, was one of Lawrence's last fictional attempts to deal with these themes.

All the new readers of that book, as well as many of those already acquainted with it, may want to know more about what Lawrence was trying to do than is always apparent in this or in his other novels when they are taken singly. The essays in the present volume are, among many other things, a vade-mecum for such readers.

The variety and scope of these selections have already been mentioned. Some of them are fairly light, though they easily slide into depths: "Cocksure Women and Hensure Men" is, for example, a scherzo treatment of the emancipated women of the 1920s, but it contains some still pertinent remarks about relations between the sexes; "Making Love to Music" is a piquant but far from shallow examination of erotic dancing, ancient and modern — and so on.

The last two essays, "Pornography and Obscenity" and "A Propos of *Lady Chatterley's Lover,*" are notable polemics which provided Judge Frederick vanPelt Bryan with some relevant citations for his enlightened court opinion (printed as appendix to this volume), which stated that the Postmaster General had acted illegally in banning *Lady Chatterley* from the United States mail. And certainly these essays are among the most searching and brilliant discussions of love and literature in relation to the meddlesomeness of censorship.

My original introduction for this volume, written before the clearing of *Lady Chatterley,* is reprinted here without change.

Taos, New Mexico
September 1959

INTRODUCTION:

D. H. Lawrence
and the "Censor-Morons"

By HARRY T. MOORE

I

Our civilization cannot afford to let the censor-moron loose. The censor-moron does not really hate anything but the living and growing human consciousness. It is our developing and extending consciousness that he threatens — and our consciousness in its newest, most sensitive activity, its vital growth. To arrest or circumscribe the vital consciousness is to produce morons, and nothing but a moron would do it.

D. H. Lawrence wrote this to Morris Ernst in an acknowledgment of Ernst's book, *To the Pure*. That was in 1928, the year in which Lawrence began to bombard English-speaking countries with the Florentine edition of his *Lady Chatterley's Lover*. Within five years Horace Gregory could say, in his *Pilgrim of the Apocalypse*, that *Lady Chatterley's Lover* had won "the half-century fight for sexual liberation in English writing," and Norman Douglas could remark, in his autobiographical *Looking Back*, that Lawrence's "beneficent, taboo-shattering bomb" had "opened a little window for the bourgeoisie." Yet, a quarter of a century after *Lady Chatterley*, no one can buy the complete text of this novel in Anglo-Saxon countries except through the black market. Meanwhile, it is ironic that *Ulysses*, which Lawrence considered an unclean book, has flourished these twenty years with legal blessing. Molly Bloom, turning drowsily in bed, can publicly rake her unpunctuative consciousness for the longest, most notably Fescennine sentence in English; but poor Connie Chatterley's awakening passion must be hugger-muggered from the policemen of the mind.

The essays in the present volume cry out for Connie's right to liberation. If Lawrence cannot speak to us as he most wanted to do, through the dramatization of a crucial problem in his novel, he can at least discuss the matter with us in the essays in the present volume, which contain his views on love, on its expression in literature, and on censorship. The most important of these

9

essays, "A Propos of *Lady Chatterley's Lover*," has long been out of print in England and has never before been published in America. Its revival now is a major publishing event.

Anyone who reads the essay will see why: it is clear, it is simple, it is profound, and it is impassioned. It explores its subject thoroughly and presents its conclusions brilliantly. Like the seven essays which accompany it here, it speaks for itself; it needs no elucidation.

This introduction, then, will confine itself to a discussion of the background of "A Propos" and of these other essays, which is also the background of Lawrence's career-long battle with the "censor-morons."

Actually, his opposition to prudery began even before his first publication. The friend of his youth, Jessie Chambers — the Miriam of his *Sons and Lovers* — recalled in her reminiscence of Lawrence that when they read Ibsen's plays aloud in their courtship days, she couldn't bring herself to utter the phrase, "keeping mistresses"; and Lawrence scolded her for "such evasions." A friend of his later life, Achsah Brewster, said in her memoir that one of Lawrence's college instructors had reprimanded him for using the word "stallion" in a class essay. Mrs. Brewster remembered that when Lawrence told her and her husband of this incident of years before, "he hung his head as if in shame for the public who could not face life."

In his youth Lawrence had to contend, at every level, with the repressive force of his mother. This former schoolteacher married to a coal miner was in every way a purist: she not only refused to learn the Midlands dialect of her husband and of her children's friends, but she even forbade the children to use it in the house. As Lawrence said in one of his poems in *Pansies,*

> indoors we called each other *you*
> outside it was *tha* and *thee*.

This mother also demanded purity of story. Jessie Chambers reported in her memoir that when Lawrence in an early draft of his first novel, *The White Peacock,* offered up his heroine to a seduction, Mrs. Lawrence "in a pained voice" lamented to Jessie, "To think that *my* son should have written such a story!" Mrs. Lawrence was too ill to read her advance copy of *The White Peacock,* and she died a month before its publication in January 1911. But in that book, which contained an idealized portrait that was a tribute to his mother, Lawrence in some passages wrote so candidly about love as to offend even his publisher, William Heinemann. In the 1890s Heinemann had been venturesome enough to publish Ibsen and Tolstoy, then regarded as "shocking" authors, but in December 1910, after *The White Peacock* had gone to the bindery, Heinemann's office rushed a copy of page 230 to Lawrence asking him, as he later recalled, to remove a paragraph which "might be considered objectionable, and substitute an exactly identical number of obviously harmless words."

Lawrence complied, in this first bout with censorship. Where he had written, "God! — we were a passionate couple — and she would have me in her bedroom while she drew Greek statues of me," he substituted, "Lord! — we were an infatuated couple — and she chose to view me in an aesthetic light. I was Greek statues for her"; and where he had said, "It took her three years to have a real bellyful of me," he later wrote, "It took her three years to be really glutted with me."

It didn't take Lawrence long to have a bellyful of — or to be really glutted with — bowdlerization, and in the future he was less willing to compromise with the advance censorship of publishers. But it was not until his fourth novel, *The Rainbow*, in 1915, that he awoke public wrath and became a banned author.

II

Some of the reviews of his earlier novels and books of poetry, however, carried hints of possible trouble. While these volumes generally received praise in the leading British and American journals, they almost invariably drew from the critics such epithets as "sensual," "decadent," "overfrank," "Zolaesque," and so on; and one reviewer seemed to believe that Lawrence was an English writer of foreign breeding. But the published work of Lawrence's which the critics saw was often a modified version of the original, for when Lawrence refused to cut down his text, the publishers sometimes did their own trimming. Occasionally they went even beyond such censorship, as when William Heinemann refused to publish *Sons and Lovers* at all. His explanation that this novel was one of the dirtiest books he had ever read, prompted Lawrence to remark, a dozen years later, "I should not have thought the deceased gentleman's reading had been so circumspectly narrow."

Duckworth published *Sons and Lovers* in 1913, and most of the reviewers praised it, though a few joined the anonymous critic of the London *Nation,* who turned away from the protagonist of the novel "in fatigued repulsion." Duckworth didn't bring out Lawrence's next novel, *The Rainbow,* because an editor of the firm, Edward Garnett, disliked the book. Garnett had been Lawrence's friend and mentor, but Lawrence refused to rewrite the manuscript as Garnett suggested. The larger house of Methuen undertook to publish it.

As Richard Aldington has observed, this book was "the product of a long patience" and "of concentrated writing and rewriting," and "no man, merely wishing to write a pornographic book, would dream of wasting so much time and energy." Yet when *The Rainbow* appeared on September 30, 1915, the critics came out screaming: it was vile and obscene, the filth outweighed the artistry, and the book was "worse than Zola" — an author who stood as a reeking symbol of pornography in the British mind because his English publisher had been fined and imprisoned. The cavil against *The Rainbow* resulted in the granting of a search warrant, on November 3, to a detective-inspector from Scotland Yard, who seized more than a thousand copies at the publishers' and at the printers'. The publishers offered no defence and spared Lawrence's feelings by not notifying him of the proceedings, which took place at Bow Street Police Court on the 13th. There a solicitor named Herbert G. Muskett, "for the Commissioner of Police," read some of the unfavorable reviews, which he reinforced with his own opinions. The publisher said he had twice sent the book back to the author for revisions, which Lawrence made and then "refused to do anything more." The publishers admitted they doubtless "acted unwisely in not scrutinizing the book more carefully, and they regretted having published it." The magistrate, Sir John Dickinson, joined in these regrets and criticized the publishers for not having suppressed the book after they had read the reviews. He ordered the seized copies "to be destroyed at the expiration of seven days (in the interim to be impounded) if no appeal," and fined the publishing house ten guineas' costs. Thus Lawrence, a poor man in a country at war, a man whose wife was "an enemy alien," became a writer whom publishers would for a long time try to avoid.

There seems to have been more than a possible violation of sex morality in this banning. May Sinclair — one of the few authors to stand up for *The Rainbow* at this time — used to say that the suppression was partly political. As Aldington remembers it, the prosecution seems to have gone so far as to suggest that the novel's implied criticisms of imperialism and of the Boer War had begun to hamper recruiting, which at that time lagged. Another friend of Lawrence's at the time, Gilbert Cannan, suggested, in an article in a New York newspaper in 1920, that war hysteria probably contributed to the suppression of *The Rainbow*. The present Commissioner of Police at New Scotland Yard has, however, said (without producing a record of the case), "The proceedings in 1915 were solely on the grounds of obscenity."

The patriotic-legal-moral criticisms of *The Rainbow* received at the time a rather weird corroboration in an article in the *Athenaeum* by a writer on popular-science subjects, G. W. de Tunzelmann. He found that Lawrence's "constant absorption in the material environment" and "its most conspicuous expression in sexual intercourse . . . glorified in itself and free from any semblance of restraint" was "but one of the many futile attempts to reconcile the facts of existence with the materialistic pseudo-philosophy which has proved such a powerful instrument for the debasement of the German nation." But this was not all, for "many of the humiliating weaknesses which have so hampered our action against Germany may be traced to the too great readiness which has been shown in accepting some of this same philosophy at the hands of those whom we are at last united in recognizing as our foes — in things spiritual as well as in things temporal." This was a ponderous burden to drape across *The Rainbow*, but George William de Tunzelmann was rather sensitive in these matters, for he had been born Georg Wilhelm von Tunzelmann. How sensitive he was to the damage he did Lawrence is not possible to determine now.

The Author's League promised to battle on behalf of *The Rainbow*, and a few of Lawrence's friends suggested that he take the matter up legally, but he lacked position and influence. One friend, however — Philip Morrell, husband of Lady Ottoline Morrell — used his status as a Liberal Member of Parliament to ask questions in the House of Commons about the suppression of the book. On November 18 he inquired whether the Home Secretary knew of the action, whether the police had Home Office authority in the matter, and whether the author "had any opportunity of replying to the charge made against him." This was easy for Sir John Simon, Secretary of State for Home Affairs and already one of the smoothest British diplomats of modern times. He pointed out that the police had acted "in pursuance of their ordinary duty," that they didn't need Home Office backing in the matter, and that the publishers had been given "the customary opportunity to produce such evidence as they considered necessary in their defence." And that was as far as Morrell was able to get. When he tried to defend the author's rights, Sir John spoke of the publishers as "the owners of what was seized." When the Home Secretary was unable to answer Morrell's question as to whether the magistrate ordering the suppression had even read the book, another Member joined the discussion: Sir Henry Craik (Unionist), representing Glasgow,

where the *Herald* had just dropped a reviewer of ten years' standing (Lawrence's friend Catherine Carswell) for writing one of the
few favorable notices of *The Rainbow*. Sir Henry blandly asked
whether "the publishers expressed extreme regret at having been
the means of publishing the book in question," and Sir John found
it easy to keep that one going: "I believe that is so, and that so far
from resisting the proceedings they said they thought it right that
the order should be issued." At this point an Irish Member inter-
vened, A. A. Lynch (Nationalist) of County Clare. He asked: "Is
there any official censor in these matters, or do these delicate
questions depend on the judgment of one magistrate?" Sir John
Simon closed the discussion by saying that there was no official
censor of literature and that he hoped there never would be one.
Certainly when officials could block an uncomfortable book as
easily as they had blocked *The Rainbow,* they didn't need an
official censor.

Two weeks later, Philip Morrell returned to the engagement.
On December 1 he again took up the matter of the rights of the
author, who he felt had been done "a grave injustice." Sir John
Simon was quick to answer, "I do not see that but however it
may be, the provisions of the law were strictly complied with, and
I feel quite certain that the magistrate would not act in a way
which was contrary to the dictates of justice." This prompted
Commander Josiah C. Wedgwood (Liberal, subsequently Labour,
and at that time home between battle-service assignments) to ask,
"Is it not monstrous that a man should have this charge levelled
against him and have no opportunity of defending himself whatsoever?" Sir John Simon, the expert conciliator, suggested that
it should be possible, "if the author thinks he was wrongly treated,
for another copy to be seized by arrangement, in order that he
might defend the book." A moment later, Sir William Byles
(Liberal) asked whether the proceedings had been "taken under
the Defence of the Realm Act" — again suggesting a political as
well as a moral censorship. "Is there any opportunity," he continued, "for the public to know what was suppressed, in order that
they might avoid getting into the clutches of the law?" Sir John
Simon reassured him that the proceedings didn't involve the Defence
of the Realm Act, but "were taken under a Statute which was
passed, I think, about 1860." The Irishman Lynch rushed in again
to ask, "Could these proceedings be taken against a classic author
who may not be living? Would it be competent, on the decision
of a police magistrate, to confiscate the works of Shakespeare,
Rabelais, Swift, and others?" — at which point the Speaker called

a halt to the discussion: "I think the Hon. Member had better give notice of that question." The intrusion of *The Rainbow* into Parliament was at an end. The Statute the Home Secretary had referred to came from deep in the Victorian age: Lord Campbell's Obscene Publications Act of 1857.

Two days after that second failure in Parliament, Lawrence told Lady Ottoline Morrell that Catherine Carswell's husband, Donald, who was a barrister, believed that Lawrence had a clear case of libel against two of the critics, and that if they acted on Sir John Simon's suggestion and had another copy seized, they could then thrash the whole matter out in court. "But my spirit will not rise to it," he said. "I can't come so near them as to fight them. I have done with them. I am not going to pay any more out of my soul, even for the sake of beating them."

He had hoped to escape to America, but he wound up in Cornwall, where for nearly two years he lived in miserable poverty, spied upon and suffering other indignities heaped upon the independent man. *The Rainbow* came out in America, bowdlerized, in 1916, but otherwise no publisher brought out a novel of Lawrence's until 1920. His poems were published in the interim (with one of the publishers, Chatto and Windus, making some excisions), and a "harmless" travel book, but except for the *English Review,* which had first printed his work, most of the magazines shunned him. His opposition to the war, as a useless waste, increased the antagonism against him, and the fact that one of his wife's cousins, Manfred von Richthofen, was the greatest of air aces — on the wrong side — didn't help either. At last, in October 1917, the authorities removed Lawrence and his wife from the coastal area, with orders for them to report regularly to the police in London. Although Lawrence had a little more police-spy trouble, he finally discovered he could return to his native Midlands, where he waited out the rest of the war, still poor and unpublished; and when he could leave England, a year after the Armistice, he did so and never again became a permanent resident there. But he was yet to give the British censors a good deal of exercise.

His first bout after *The Rainbow*, however, was with American Comstockery. A new publisher, Thomas Seltzer, brought out the sequel to *The Rainbow, Women in Love,* in a subscribers' edition in November 1920, after it had gone begging for nearly four years; then Seltzer published it in the regular way in 1922. Trouble began one evening when Justice John Ford of the New York Supreme Court came home to his West 86th Street apartment and found his daughter reading *Women in Love*. The judge, an expert on protective tariff, decided that another kind of protection was in order. He organized the Clean Books League, whose object was to make the law against "obscene" books — in the language of this legal-minded native of Knowlesville, N. Y., "horse-high, pig-tight, and bull-strong." That would stop this "saturnalia of obscenity"! He persuaded John S. Sumner and his New York Society for the Suppression of Vice to go after *Women in Love,* but Sumner's onslaught was a failure. On September 22, 1922, Lawrence, then living in the United States, wrote Earl Brewster: "Seltzer had a case: the 'Vice' people tried to suppress *Women in Love* and other books: Seltzer won completely, and is now claiming $10,000 damages." The "horse-high, pig-tight" people had lost their case ten days before, when Gilbert Seldes, Dorothea Brande, Carl Van Doren, and several New York doctors had defended *Women in Love* along with a Schnitzler novel and a book with an introduction by Freud. Magistrate George W. Simpson found that Lawrence was seriously attempting to "discover the motivating power of life."

And, as the world grew farther away from the conformism of war, braces relaxed; for a time there was a kind of shaky freedom. In March 1921, the Oxford University Press regarded Lawrence as a sufficiently good author to provide them with a textbook, *Movements in European History,* but also as a sufficient liability to use the pseudonym "Lawrence H. Davison" on the title page. The previous year, however, Martin Secker had published Lawrence's fifth novel, *The Lost Girl,* in London — after removing a few passages — and it won the James Tait Black Memorial Prize of one hundred pounds, given by Edinburgh University for the "best" novel of the year. Secker ventured *Women in Love* in May 1921, and then the screaming began again. The loudest was from the loudest of the London papers, Horatio Bottomley's *John Bull,* whose headline shrieked, "A Book The Police Should Ban," and whose sub-title shrilled, "Loathsome Study of Sex Depravity — Misleading Youth to Unspeakable Disaster." But by November, Lawrence could write a chuckling note to Brewster: "Bottomley is in such a dirty mess himself, having swindled half England . . . and being on trial for weeks, that he is not going to be allowed to suppress *Women in Love.*" And although several of the more "dignified" journals continued the complaint, no one suppressed the book. The only threats of trouble came from those who had been caricatured in it, among them Philip Heseltine (the composer "Peter Warlock"), who threatened Secker with a libel suit on account of the portrait of Halliday, and in the next edition Lawrence had to give this character a wig of another color.

As the twenties swung on, judges became more liberal and fewer books were legally banned. Flimsy novels such as *Jurgen* and *The Well of Loneliness* won some of the battles waged in their behalf, and by 1933 the plea of Morris Ernst and the decision of Judge Woolsey had given a truly significant novel, *Ulysses*, the right to be free. By the 1950s, cold-war terrors encouraged the censors to go hunting again, for books both good and bad — the difference to most censors is inconsequential or, in most cases, unrecognized.

Lawrence had trouble with them, however, before the twenties were over. Some of his battles were private rather than public. In May 1925, for example, the Oxford University Press issued a new edition of the *European History*, at last acknowledging Lawrence as the author. But in November these publishers asked him to make some changes for an edition aimed at the Irish school market, and in a letter from Spotorno, Italy (as yet unpublished), Lawrence complained to one of the editors of the press about his "mauled edition." Making the deletions had both amused and infuriated him, he said: he asked that the copy he had marked be returned to him, to serve as a stimulus for his bile and as a reminder of the glory of the human race.

That race had not, incidentally, been altogether neglecting Lawrence. Although a minority author, little praised by critics an reviewers, he had in some years of the 1920s an annual income of about $5000 — good money in those times, particularly for a frugal man. His only heavy expenses were for transportation: his restless travels over the globe in search of health and peace of mind.

On those wanderings he had plenty of opportunity to observe the human race in all its important manifestations; and he did not like much of what he saw. But a good part of Lawrence's criticism of all modern life came out of his earliest experiences. As a child he had seen how the regimentation of industrialism could damage individuals and families; and as he was growing up amid the remnants of Sherwood Forest, he had seen the smoke from the collieries blemish the landscape that had once been so beautiful. He had seen too how the mechanization of life had invaded the province of the emotions and how it was killing them, especially the most vital, that of love. He sought for remedies, and in the 1920s examined the competing social philosophies of the time — such as fascism and communism — and in rejecting them made some profound and important criticisms of them. He wished at times to reject democracy, perhaps because he was too involved in that system to realize that only a democracy, "censor-morons" and all, can make a D. H. Lawrence possible. If democracy seemed to reject Lawrence, it was at the worst only a partial rejection, for even though fools may outnumber wise men, it is the latter who have, in democracy, often prevailed. The survival of Lawrence helps to prove this: a few of the Old Guard still snipe at him from what is left of the Victorian shrubbery, but for the most part the response has changed, and he is almost universally regarded now as being among the great English authors. Yet, as previously mentioned, no one has yet dared to publish *Lady Chatterley's Lover* in any of the Anglo-Saxon countries.

That book contains one of the most vital statements of his message. He had wearied of attempts at "leadership," of theorizing about politics, and of efforts to set up a Utopian colony; he had above all discovered, as the title of one of his essays of the time shows, that "We Need One Another." Love was the answer: passionate love, not willed or mentally controlled love — the product of a crippling civilization — but a love that would burn out shame and all other hampering elements. Lawrence himself can best explain these matters, as he does in the essays in the present volume.

His essays and "philosophy" always came after he had worked out his ideas in fiction or poetry. As he said in the Foreword to his *Fantasia of the Unconscious* (1922), "The novels and poems come unwatched out of one's pen. And then the absolute need which one has for some sort of satisfactory mental attitude towards oneself and things in general make one try to abstract some definite conclusions from one's experiences as a writer and a man."

Did *Lady Chatterley's Lover* "come unwatched out of [his] pen?" It did, according to Lawrence's testimony in "A Propos": "When I created Clifford and Connie, I had no idea what they were or why they were. They just came, pretty much as they are." But he changed the character of the gamekeeper, Mellors (originally Parkin), as he wrote his three drafts of the book, from late 1926 to early 1928. Parkin had been, in the first version, more of a "social" figure; with Mellors, in the third, the social motif was implicit rather than direct, thereby emphasizing the love theme more exclusively.

Lawrence knew he was going to have censor trouble with this book. His publishers refused even to consider bringing it out and his agents would not attempt to place it. He finally published it himself, with the help of the Florentine bookseller Giuseppe Orioli; they had the book printed in a little shop where the com-

positor knew no English and made some typographical howlers
that amused Lawrence: "He writes dind't, did'nt, dnid't, dind't,
didn't like a Bach fugue." Lawrence, as he explains in "A Propos,"
had warned the printer as to what the book said in English, and
the printer had shrugged it off with "O! *ma!* but we do it every
day!" Lawrence knew of the agony that lay ahead; Frieda recalls
that he was "scared," yet had the courage to proceed anyhow.

Lady Chatterley was a profitable venture for Lawrence, for
subscribers soon absorbed the first edition of a thousand copies at
two guineas each. Later editions likewise sold well, though the
pirates cut in on Lawrence's profits, particularly in the United
States. The book had no copyright, and the pirates printed their
own editions; in English-speaking countries *Lady Chatterley* has
remained a black-market staple.

Even though the book may have helped Lawrence financially,
it damaged his health. It is probable that the strain of *Lady
Chatterley's Lover* — not so much of the writing as of the fretting
over publication details and over censorship — hastened his death.
Lawrence fretted over these small matters, during 1928 and 1929,
when he was ill in the Swiss Alps and on the Mediterranean French
coast. He received letters from all kinds of people about his novel.
Booksellers, critics, and general readers wrote him, most of them
inquiring about *Lady Chatterley* or complaining because their
orders had gone astray. Lawrence scribbled answers in the margins
or on the backs of their letters and sent these to Orioli for formal
typed reply: it is ironic that one of the most prolifically creative
authors of our time, a sick man, too, should have written more
business letters than any of his peers, except perhaps the insurance
clerk Kafka and the publisher Eliot.

Lawrence during the distribution of *Lady Chatterley* continued
writing his poems, articles, and stories, and also kept up his abun-
dant correspondence with friends. He particularly had to remain
in close touch with those in England — Richard Aldington, S. S.
Koteliansky, Enid Hilton, Brigit Patmore — who hid smuggled
copies of *Lady Chatterley* in their London flats or country cottages,
mailing them to subscribers in England who had sent their orders,
as prescribed, to Florence. The book had poorer luck in America,
not only because of the pirates but also because of the New York
customs officers: Lawrence suspected these men of pretending to
confiscate the copies and then selling them on the sly for twice the
announced cost. Lawrence tried to work out various dodges, such
as having the Florentine printer manufacture some false jackets
(*The Way of All Flesh,* by Samuel Butler — and so on) and in-

structing Orioli to put those on some of the books and try mailing
them via Galveston and New Orleans. Meanwhile, the old enemy
John Bull, in spite of the downfall of Bottomley, continued to rage
against Lawrence: "Shameful Book — A Landmark in Evil," the
headlines blared, and an article explained that *Lady Chatterley's
Lover* was "the most evil outpouring that has ever besmirched the
literature of our country. The sewers of French pornography would
be dragged in vain to find a parallel in beastliness." Most of the
other papers took the same attitude, though not quite the same tone.

Lawrence's official enemies meanwhile sharpened their eyes.
Stanley Baldwin's Home Secretary, Sir William Joynson-Hicks
("Jix"), believed, although there was still no official censor for
books, that "the Government has a general responsibility for the
moral welfare of the community," and he spoke of "the duty inherent in all Governments of combating such dangers as threaten
the safety or well-being of the State." These platitudes he over-
simplified in his daily activities to signify that Lawrence was one
of the dangers to the safety and well-being of the State; he made
it plain that he was out to "get" Lawrence. Customs officers, postal
clerks, and Scotland Yard inspectors apparently were put on the
alert for his books or manuscripts in the mails.

On January 7, 1929, at Bandol in Southern France, Lawrence
registered the manuscript of his *Pansies* poems as *papiers d'affaires,*
No. 587, and mailed them to his agent in London. To the joy of
Jix, these fell into the hands of Scotland Yard. A week later they
also laid hold of the introduction to the volume of Lawrence's
paintings which the Mandrake Press planned to issue in London.
Again Lawrence had defenders: Ellen Wilkinson and other Labour
MP's asked questions in Parliament about the seizure. The Home
Secretary — still Jix, who that year became Viscount Brentford —
told his inquirers that he didn't "seek literary advice when deciding
if matter was obscene." Eventually he turned the manuscripts over
to the publishers with the recommendation that fourteen of the
poems be omitted; and in July 1929 Martin Secker published the
book with these poems left out. Lawrence, however, had a friend
print him a special unexpurgated edition, dated June but not re-
leased till August, of five hundred copies (plus fifty on Japanese
vellum), of which Lawrence signed the verso of the title page.
Pansies was not one of his most important books; the poems were
satiric doggerel, sometimes amusing, sometimes wearying, but Jix
by his tactics helped give them a special *réclame,* and the venture
apparently brought Lawrence five hundred pounds for the limited
edition alone. That was later reprinted on the Continent, from the

same plates, in a popular edition. It has never been published in America; Knopf's New York edition in September 1929 duplicated the eviscerated Secker version.

It was in that same year of 1929 that Lawrence's paintings brought about another wrangle with the censors, less than a year before his death. After his exhibition of paintings opened at the Warren Gallery, in Mayfair, Frieda Lawrence went to London to see the show, while Lawrence visited the Aldous Huxleys in Italy. The exhibition opened on June 14, coincident with the publication date of the colored reproductions of Lawrence's pictures, and before the police closed it on July 5, some twelve thousand people had come to see the paintings. This time it was the turn of the art critics to be hostile, as most of them were; like so many of the literary critics they attacked Lawrence's work on both aesthetic and moral grounds.

Jix was not the Home Secretary at the time of the closing of the exhibition, however, for Jix had gone out of office when the Conservative Government lost the May elections. His Labour Government successor, John Robert Clynes, was no more helpful. He was Home Secretary on that July day when two policemen — an inspector and a sergeant — expressed horror at what they saw at the gallery. They came back later in the day, with authority and reinforcements, and removed thirteen paintings, as well as four copies of the Mandrake Press's book of reproductions which they discovered. They also started to make off with a volume of Blake's drawings, but on learning that this artist had been dead for a century and two years, they decided not to disturb *his* book. Another volume, translated by Louis Aragon into the immoral French language, looked suspicious, but the policemen decided not to take it after the owners of the gallery explained to them that *The Hunting of the Snark* was a children's classic. They did, however, impound a volume of drawings by Georg Grosz, thereby antedating Hitler as an art critic.

The case against the paintings was heard on August 8, at Marlborough Street police court, before Magistrate Frederick Mead, aged eighty-two. The *Rainbow* prosecutor, Herbert G. Muskett, again appeared, this time to characterize the pictures as "gross, coarse, hideous, unlovely, and obscene." Experts whom the defence wished to call — Augustus John, Sir William Orpen, Arnold Bennett, Glyn Philpot, and others — were not allowed to testify. Speaking of the paintings, the ancient magistrate said, "It is utterly immaterial whether they are works of art or not. The most splendidly painted picture in the universe might be obscene." And obscene pictures should be "put an end to, like any wild animal which may be dangerous."

Magistrate Mead never exactly pronounced the paintings obscene, though the warrant had been issued under the same Act of 1857 under which an earlier protector of the people had condemned *The Rainbow*. Apparently the seizure of the paintings in 1929 marked the first invocation of that Act in relation to an art gallery. There was talk of burning the pictures, which were stored in the cellar of the police station. Frieda Lawrence worried lest the dampness ruin them there, but finally the magistrate allowed the proprietors of the gallery to take them away on condition that they would not be exhibited again. Lawrence, who had been ill in Italy, cursed his fellow countrymen, whom he was never to see again on their own land.

In a volume of stinging little doggerel verses he called *Nettles,* Lawrence satirized the art critics, the censors, and the Great British Public. One of his lawyers at the hearing had complained because a "so-called advanced government" had permitted such censorship as the seizure of the pictures. Lawrence in his *Nettles* poem "Change of Government" found that

> Auntie Maud has come to keep house
> instead of Auntie Gwendolen,

while in an article in an American magazine, Aldous Huxley phrased it, *"La Grundy est morte. Vive la Grundy!"* Huxley's attack on the suppression of the pictures appeared in the November 1929 *Vanity Fair,* two months after Rebecca West's discussion of the matter in another American magazine, the *Bookman*. Rebecca West, harshly critical of some of the paintings, had praised a few of them and said that their impounding by the police was "an appalling indiscretion, considering that Mr. D. H. Lawrence is perhaps the greatest genius of these times, and so ridiculously sensitive that this is likely as not to cause a temporary paralysis of his work."

Despite such statements, however, censors and policemen in America showed as little concern for Lawrence's feelings in the matter as such people showed elsewhere. The New England Watch and Ward Society was particularly alert to damage Lawrence, and that winter they succeeded. One of their agents, whose name actually seems to have been John T. Slaymaker, pretended that he was interested in literature and went to Dunster House Bookshop, in Cambridge, Massachusetts, and asked for a copy of *Lady Chatterley*. Slaymaker was a man of sixty, and we may imagine his discreet Bostonian whisper of the speakeasy epoch, as he asked for the forbidden volume. He was warned that it was on sale for scholars rather than the general public, and it was as an ostensible scholar that he purchased the book. He proudly returned to the Watch and Ward headquarters with his prize. The manager of the bookshop was called into court on November 25, convicted of selling obscene literature, fined $800, and sentenced to four months in the House of Correction; a clerk from the store was fined $200 and sentenced to two weeks' imprisonment.

They appealed, and their case came up in Superior Court on December 19 and 20, 1929, before Judge Fosdick. The defense attorney, Herbert Parker, called the Watch and Ward Society "deceivers" and "falsifiers" and "depraved and perverted procurers." Since he was defending the booksellers rather than Lawrence, he made no attempt to defend *Lady Chatterley's Lover;* indeed, he and the prosecutor and the judge all agreed that the book was "obscene." What made the case unusual was the attack the prosecutor, Robert T. Bushnell, made upon those who had brought him the evidence:

I want the public to understand that the district attorney does not endorse the Watch and Ward Society's policy or tactics. I serve warning here and now that as long as I am district attorney of this district and the agents of this Society go into a bookstore of good repute and induce and procure the commission of a crime, I will proceed against them for criminal conspiracy.

The judge joined the district attorney in censuring the Watch and Ward Society, but said that under the law the defendants were guilty and their sentence must stand.

The increasing attacks against Lawrence may have helped crush the life out of him. The trouble over the pictures left him bitter and ill, and one day in the South of France not long before his death in 1930, Lawrence tapped his chest while talking to Earl Brewster, and said, "The hatred which my books have aroused comes back at me and gets me here."

III

The history of Lawrence and the censors does not stop, however, with his death, for even after all these years the salient issues have not been settled. Yet, as T. S. Eliot once said, Lawrence has had more influence on his time than any of his contemporaries. In 1933, only three years after Lawrence's death, Norman Douglas, who cared little for Lawrence's work, could say, in a book quoted at the beginning of this Introduction, "An American friend tells me that Lawrence's romances have been of incalculable service to genteel society out there. The same applies to genteel society in England." And, as also noted earlier, in that same year the American poet Horace Gregory pointed out that, because of *Lady Chatterley's Lover,* "no novelist (or poet) living today finds it necessary to continue the half-century fight for sexual liberation in English writing."

Yet there is a bad side to the situation, too. In blasting open the road to tolerance, Lawrence accidentally made it possible for a number of fifth-raters to come skidding along after him. It would be unfair to blame him for all the shoddy sex novels now available, for such literature has always been with us — he gave it no ancestry. Nevertheless, some of the sensational covers seen on the paperbound books in the drugstores of America may, however faintly, derive somewhat from *Lady Chatterley's Lover,* if only because their authors have hoped that they can imitate that book, not realizing that the essence of *Lady Chatterley's Lover* is an unflinching candor rather than the suggestion — or suggestiveness — apparently indispensable to the pharmacy paperbacks. Regrettably, the title *Lady Chatterley's Lover* is among those paperbacks, and it has also appeared in other cheap editions in England and America over the last twenty years. These editions are "authorized" — but not by Lawrence. He describes in "A Propos" how he tried to cut the book to please the publishers, but couldn't do so. The publishers "authorized" the emasculated version after his death. There was nothing wrong, however, in the idea of publishing *The First Lady Chatterley* in 1944, for there was respectable literary opinion to the effect that this version was at least as good as if not better than the third draft which Lawrence himself had published; but the book-policemen seemed to think it a bad idea despite its lack of the four-letter words that had stirred up so much hatred and terror of that previous edition. On May 9, 1944, the indefatigable Charles S. Sumner raided the New York office of the Dial Press and seized four hundred copies. Twenty days later a magistrate duly pronounced the book obscene, but on November 2, two of the three justices in the Court of Special Sessions declared that there was "reasonable doubt" as to obscenity and dismissed the case against *The First Lady Chatterley.*

Now, twenty years after the legalization of *Ulysses,* we might expect a publisher to undertake the genuine *Lady Chatterley's Lover. Ulysses* was cleared because it was a work of art — it reflected life, and if life is sordid at times, art must be also. Lawrence would never have accepted this defence of *Ulysses,* which to him represented a mechanization of the vital forces of life; it appealed too exclusively to the intellect. Joyce's devices seemed to Lawrence tiresome and "dirty-minded": how he must have loathed the elaborate description of Mr. Bloom's early-morning pleasure in his back-garden reading room, the manifestation of his later tribute to Gertie McDowell, indeed the entire day's catalogue of voyeurism, frottage, and various other kinds of aberrant gratification. Lawrence's horror at this type of literature, at this kind of vision of life, the reader may find expressed in "Pornography and Obscenity," in the passage where Lawrence explains how "the sex functions and the excretory functions in the human body" are "utterly different": the one is the creative flow, the other is the "flow towards dissolution, decreation, if we may use such a word." Lawrence pointed out further that "in the really healthy human being the distinction between the two is instant. . . . But in the degraded human being the deep instincts have gone dead, and then the two flows become identical."

That is so clear that it cannot be misunderstood; and of course the essay in which it appeared is required reading for all who presume to write on Lawrence. Yet the prejudice against him is deep in the hearts of those who have determined to set themselves against him.* A few years ago, in reviewing a book on Lawrence for the New York *Herald Tribune,* Professor DeLancey Ferguson said that Lawrence's "constant preoccupation with the physical mechanisms of sex and excretion is certainly proof of emotional immaturity." Frieda Lawrence wrote the *Herald Tribune* in protest. Part of her letter appeared in that paper, and it is extremely pertinent:

Lawrence wrote about almost everything under the sun, he also wrote about sex. Considering sex is the very root of our existence, without it we could not walk on this earth, it seems worthy of any mature man's thought as much as any atom bomb. Lawrence tried to raise sex from a mere animal function to a truly human all-embracing activity. Where in all Lawrence's work did Professor Ferguson discover any possible reference to a preoccupation with *excrement!* It is an ugly invention!

* Some readers only partly familiar with Lawrence's writings may be baffled by such passages as the one in *Lady Chatterley's Lover* in which the lover celebrates the beloved because she functions naturally. Such passages are too rare in Lawrence to constitute an "obsession"; and in any event, Lawrence in that part of his novel was dramatizing, in a positive way, a point he discusses in the essays in the present volume: see his references, in his *Pansies* Introduction and in his "A Propos" essay, to Swift's poem "To a Lady's Dressing-Room." Lawrence in these references discovers such an obsession in Swift and probes its cause; in *Lady Chatterley's Lover,* Lawrence attempted to show us how to cure such a condition. But probably those who only half-read an author's texts will still insist upon their right to misunderstand Lawrence. [H.T.M.]

Mrs. Lawrence added a thought — which the newspaper did not print — to the effect that she suspected that Mr. Ferguson was a young man whose later experience would teach him much about life, including "a little intelligent respect for his betters." Mrs. Lawrence of course didn't know that Mr. Ferguson is a well-known scholar, critic, and editor, author of several books, and chairman of an English Department.

Pressed to prove his point, he told Irita Van Doren, editor of the Book Review section of the *Herald Tribune,* that she would hardly care to print the texts on which he had "based the remark which has caused most of the shooting and shouting." The inhibitions of newspapers, he said, would prevent him from defending himself. But what prevented Mr. Ferguson from observing the usual practices of scholarship in regard to texts which for reasons of copyright, length, or "obscenity" cannot be reproduced — what prevented him from referring to page and line numbers of the supposed passages?

Fortunately, most of Mr. Ferguson's colleagues apparently do not share his feelings about Lawrence; teachers of literature, many of them publishing literary critics, have played an important role in the Lawrence revival. Yet, even though *Lady Chatterley* may have gained a bit of academic respectability, the book is still subject to the kind of distortion that William York Tindall mentions in the Introduction to his excellent anthology, *The Later D. H. Lawrence* (1952). Professor Tindall says that "there are tales of couples reading Lawrence on couches: putting him aside to lie on them." But the essays in the present volume make it plain that Lawrence did not write his books for the titillation of suburban Paolos and Francescas — nor, as some of his apologists in the recent *Lady Chatterley* trial in Japan tried to explain, for the practical encouragement of adulteries under the almond blossoms and cherry trees.

That trial is one of the most interesting chapters in the history of Lawrence's battle with the censors. Translated into Japanese by Sei Ito of Waseda University, the unexpurgated edition of *Lady Chatterley's Lover* appeared in Tokyo in the spring of 1950. Immediately lawyers, publishers, civic leaders, authors, journalists, professors, and a good many plain readers collaborated to produce one of the greatest uproars heard in Japan since the end of the war. Trials in 1952 and 1953 resulted in the conviction and fining of the publisher, Hisajiro Koyama, against whom the prosecution drew up an impressive list of witnesses, including the president of the Society for the Reform of Manners, the chairman of the Committee on the Regulation and Control of Cinema Ethics, the chief of the Diet Library, the presidents of several girls' schools, the president of the Mothers' Society of Kanda, a Yokohama Medical College professor and, among others, "Mr. Sinnosuke Abe, a publicist." Those who would point a Gilbert and Sullivan finger at these proceedings should recall some of those of the Western World, as previously described. The elder generation of Japanese had been disturbed, the trial brought out, by "the trend of the times," and the prosecution of *Lady Chatterley* was only one among more than a hundred such cases tried since the war — though of course the most spectacular one. And if the trial had its comic aspects, well, sex has always been a subject that has thrown people off center — even the poised ancients.

In the modern world Lawrence had discerned and was trying to correct the present-day imbalance between intellectual and emotional elements, not only in sex but in all other phases of human life. He stressed passion and the emotions because humanity had so long neglected them: he was not trying to destroy the intellectual processes, but merely to bring them into their proper relationship with the emotions.

Fortunately, everyone has not misunderstood and reviled Lawrence and his message. One of those who exactly comprehended what D. H. Lawrence was trying to do was the late T. E. Lawrence ("of Arabia"); he had on first reading been a bit put off by *Lady Chatterley,* but at last he came to the understanding expressed in his letter of March 3, 1930, to the effect that the meaning of *Lady Chatterley* "is that the idea of sex, and the whole strong vital instinct, being considered indecent causes men to lose what might be their vital strength and pride of life — their integrity. . . . Ironically, or paradoxically, in a humanity where [in Blake's sense] 'genitals are beauty' there would be a minimum of 'sex' and a maximum of beauty, or Art. This is what Lawrence means, surely." In a scientific, philological study of the most famous of all taboo words, Allen Walker Read's article "An Obscenity Symbol," in *American Speech* for December 1934, said: "A courageous attempt to ignore the taboo was made by D. H. Lawrence in his novel *Lady Chatterley's Lover.* His use of the word in sincere simplicity differs strikingly from the inverted taboo of those who trade upon sex as a dirty secret." Professor Read regretted, however, that the taboo words were still so shocking in their "smirched associations" that Lawrence's "experiment, admirable in aim," failed with most people — but perhaps that condition now is changing. The words have been so widely used that they are less shocking today: and if people can understand Lawrence's use of them, his books will be read at last as they should be read — indeed, as many people have begun to read them. Most recently, Lawrence's old friend Aldous Huxley, in *The Devils of Loudon,* published in 1952, made a passing reference to "the sexuality of Eden and the sexuality of the sewer," pointing out that "there is an element in sexuality which is innocent, and there is an element in sexuality which is morally and aesthetically squalid. . . . Jean Genet, with horrifying power and copious detail," has dealt with the latter, while "D. H. Lawrence has written very beautifully of the first," the sexuality of Eden.

IV

The present essays are a by-product of Lawrence's imaginative writing. As we have seen, creation with him preceded explanation. Yet if the reprinting of these explanations can bring about the reprinting of the creations — specifically *Lady Chatterley's Lover* — they will have served a good purpose. Nevertheless they have a wider application as well, for they are at the top of all discussions of this perplexing and important subject.

The first of these essays, in order of composition, is "Love." Its first publication was in the *English Review* for January 1918. Lawrence perhaps wrote it during the preceding year, before his expulsion from Cornwall in October. It is one of the most important statements he made about love and it was made in the middle of his career; reproduced in the *Phoenix* volume, it has long been out of print in America. In 1925 Lawrence published several other important essays on love and sex, in *Reflections on the Death of a Porcupine,* but since the best of these have recently come back into print, they are not reprinted in the present collection of material which has been too long inaccessible.

The second of these essays in point of time, "Making Love to Music," followed its predecessor by about ten years. The note at the end of the manuscript — April 26, 1927 — apparently dates its composition exactly. The essay first appeared in *Phoenix: The Posthumous Papers of D. H. Lawrence* (1936), and like many of the essays in that volume it has for some years been out of print in both England and America.

Apparently written about August 1928, "Cocksure Women and Hensure Men" received first publication the following January in the *Forum* (New York), in which Lawrence had previously ruffled the readers' feathers with the opening section of his novel, *The Escaped Cock.* Lawrence had predicted that the English magazines would reject his "Cocksure" essay, a prophecy which proved true. He put the essay into his *Assorted Articles* volume, however, where it appeared in April 1930, a month after his death.

"Sex versus Loveliness" first appeared in the *Sunday Dispatch* (London) on November 25, 1928, as "Sex Locked Out," and on the following July in *Vanity Fair* (New York) as "Sex Appeal" — a phrase Lawrence disliked. He changed the title to "Sex versus Loveliness" for *Assorted Articles*.

The manuscript of the "Introduction to *Pansies*" Lawrence dated "Bandol, Christmas 1929." After the seizure of the *Pansies* manuscript, Lawrence wrote a new Introduction; in the limited edition of *Pansies* the date at the end of this Introduction is January 1929. A somewhat different preface appeared in the trade edition. The "limited" Introduction, reprinted in *Phoenix* and in the present volume, represents the first expression of some of the most important thoughts developed in the two longer essays at the end of this book.

"The State of Funk" was written perhaps in late 1928 or early 1929. It first appeared in print in *Assorted Articles*. Like the other two essays reproduced here from that volume, it has long been out of print in America.

Lawrence wrote "Pornography and Obscenity" at Rottach-am-Tegernsee, Bavaria, where he stayed from late August to mid-September of 1929, as guest of Max Mohr, German physician and playwright, to whom he wrote from Bandol on December 19, 1929: "That *Obscenity* pamphlet which I wrote at Rottach, at the Angermeister, has made the old ones hate me still more in England, but it has sold very well, and had a very good effect, I think." Lawrence later rejoiced that it considerably outsold the pamphlet in the same series written by Jix. Faber and Faber had brought out Lawrence's "Pornography" essay as Number 5 of the Criterion Miscellany, in London, in November; Knopf issued it in New York in 1930.

"A Propos of *Lady Chatterley's Lover*" is the extension of the Introduction to the authorized 1929 Paris edition of *Lady Chatterley's Lover*. This Introduction, "My Skirmish with a Jolly Roger," was issued in a limited edition (of twelve pages) by Random House, in New York, in July 1929. Later, apparently at Bandol in the fall of 1929, Lawrence increased its length to some sixty pages; Mandrake Press published the result, with the title used in this volume, in London in June 1930; Heinemann brought it out a few years later, but its appearance in the present volume marks its first in America.

As previously stated, these essays do not need explication. Law-

rence's views about sex were based on common sense and on the
wisdom of a great writer who looked into the heart of life and
could report his findings brilliantly. And certainly, in these days
of quasi-legal inquisition and of the triumphant braying of all
reactionaries, Lawrence's attacks on the "censor-moron" are more
necessary and important than ever. Taken together, the essays in
this book might be said to comprise a twentieth-century *Areo-
pagitica* for the literature of love.

Wellesley Hills, Massachusetts
Easter, 1953

Sex,
Literature,
and Censorship

Love

Love is the happiness of the world. But happiness is not the whole of fulfilment. Love is a coming together. But there can be no coming together without an equivalent going asunder. In love, all things unite in a oneness of joy and praise. But they could not unite unless they were previously apart. And, having united in a whole circle of unity, they can go no further in love. The motion of love, like a tide, is fulfilled in this instance; there must be an ebb.

So that the coming together depends on the going apart; the systole depends on the diastole; the flow depends upon the ebb. There can never be love universal and unbroken. The sea can never rise to high tide over all the globe at once. The undisputed reign of love can never be.

Because love is strictly a travelling. "It is better to travel than to arrive," somebody has said. This is the essence of unbelief. It is a belief in absolute love, when love is by nature relative. It is a belief in the means, but not in the end. It is strictly a belief in force, for love is a unifying force.

How shall we believe in force? Force is instrumental and functional; it is neither a beginning nor an end. We travel in order to arrive; we do not travel in order to travel. At least, such travelling is mere futility. We travel in order to arrive.

And love is a travelling, a motion, a speed of coming together. Love is the force of creation. But all force, spiritual or physical, has its polarity, its positive and its negative. All things that fall, fall by gravitation to the earth. But has not the earth, in the opposite of gravitation, cast off the moon and held her at bay in our heavens during all the aeons of time?

So with love. Love is the hastening gravitation of spirit towards spirit, and body towards body, in the joy of creation. But if all be united in one bond of love, then there is no more love. And therefore, for those who are in love with love, to travel is better than to arrive. For in arriving one passes beyond love, or, rather, one encompasses love in a new transcendence. To arrive is the supreme joy after all our travelling.

The bond of love! What worse bondage can we conceive than the bond of love? It is an attempt to wall in the high tide; it is a will to arrest the spring, never to let May dissolve into June, never to let the hawthorn petal fall for the berrying.

This has been our idea of immortality, this infinite of love, love universal and triumphant. And what is this but a prison and a bondage? What is eternity but the endless passage of time? What is infinity but an endless progressing through space? Eternity, infinity, our great ideas of rest and arrival, what are they but ideas of endless travelling? Eternity is the endless travelling through space; no more, however we try to argue it. And immortality, what is it, in our idea, but an endless continuing in the same sort? A continuing, a living forever, a lasting and enduring forever — what is this but travelling? An assumption into heaven, a becoming one with God — what is the infinite on arrival? The infinite is no arrival. When we come to find exactly what we mean by God, by the infinite, by our immortality, it is a meaning of endless continuing in the same line and in the same sort, endless travelling in one direction. This is infinity, endless travelling in one direction. And the God of Love is our idea of the progression *ad infinitum* of the force of love. Infinity is no arrival. It is as much a cul-de-sac as is the bottomless pit. And what is the infinity of love but a cul-de-sac or a bottomless pit?

Love is a progression towards the goal. Therefore it is a progression away from the opposite goal. Love travels heavenwards. What then does love depart from? Hellwards, what is there? Love is at last a positive infinite. What then is the negative infinite? Positive and negative infinite are the same, since there is only one infinite. How then will it matter if we travel heavenwards, *ad infinitum,* or in the opposite direction, to infinity? Since the infinity obtained is the same in either case, the infinite of pure homogeneity, which is nothingness, or everythingness, it does not matter which.

Infinity, the infinite, is no goal. It is a cul-de-sac, or, in another sense, it is the bottomless pit. To fall down the bottomless pit is to travel forever. And a pleasant-walled cul-de-sac may be a perfect heaven. But to arrive in a sheltered, paradisiacal cul-de-sac of peace and unblemished happiness, this will not satisfy us. And to fall forever down the bottomless pit of progression, this will not do either.

Love is not a goal; it is only a travelling. Likewise death is not a goal; it is a travelling asunder into elemental chaos. And from the elemental chaos all is cast forth again into creation. Therefore death also is but a cul-de-sac, a melting-pot.

There is a goal, but the goal is neither love nor death. It is a goal neither infinite nor eternal. It is the realm of calm delight, it is the other-kingdom of bliss. We are like a rose, which is a miracle of pure centrality, pure absolved equilibrium. Balanced in perfection in the midst of time and space, the rose is perfect in the realm of perfection, neither temporal nor spatial, but absolved by the quality of perfection, pure immanence of absolution.

We are creatures of time and space. But we are like a rose; we accomplish perfection, we arrive in the absolute. We are creatures of time and space. And we are at once creatures of pure transcendence, absolved from time and space, perfected in the realm of the absolute, the other-world of bliss.

And love, love is encompassed and surpassed. Love always has been encompassed and surpassed by the fine lovers. We are like a rose, a perfect arrival.

Love is manifold, it is not of one sort only. There is the love between man and woman, sacred and profane. There is Christian love, "thou shalt love thy neighbor as thyself." And there is the love of God. But always love is a joining together.

Only in the conjunction of man and woman has love kept a duality of meaning. Sacred love and profane love, they are opposed, and yet they are both love. The love between man and woman is the greatest and most complete passion the world will ever see, because it is dual, because it is of two opposing kinds. The love between man and woman is the perfect heart-beat of life, systole, diastole.

Sacred love is selfless, seeking not its own. The lover serves his beloved and seeks perfect communion of oneness with her. But whole love between man and woman is sacred and profane together. Profane love seeks its own. I seek my own in the beloved, I wrestle with her to wrest it from her. We are not clear, we are mixed and mingled. I am in the beloved also, and she is in me. Which should not be, for this is confusion and chaos. Therefore I will gather myself complete and free from the beloved, she shall single herself out in utter contradistinction to me. There is twilight in our souls, neither light nor dark. The light must draw itself together in purity, the dark must stand on the other hand; they must be two complete in opposition, neither one partaking of the other, but each single in its own stead.

We are like a rose. In the pure passion for oneness, in the

pure passion for distinctness and separateness, a dual passion of
unutterable separation and lovely conjunction of the two, the new
configuration takes place, the transcendence, the two in their perfect singleness, transported into one surpassing heaven of a rose
blossom.

But the love between a man and a woman, when it is whole,
is dual. It is the melting into pure communion, and it is the friction of sheer sensuality, both. In pure communion I become whole
in love. And in pure, fierce passion of sensuality I am burned into
essentiality. I am driven from the matrix into sheer separate distinction. I become my single self, inviolable and unique, as the gems
were perhaps once driven into themselves out of the confusion of
earths. The woman and I, we are the confusion of earths. Then in
the fire of their extreme sensual love, in the friction of intense,
destructive flames, I am destroyed and reduced to her essential
otherness. It is a destructive fire, the profane love. But it is the only
fire that will purify us into singleness, fuse us from the chaos into
our own unique gem-like separateness of being.

All whole love between man and woman is thus dual, a love
which is the motion of melting, fusing together into oneness, and
a love which is the intense, frictional, and sensual gratification
of being burnt down, burnt apart into separate clarity of being;
unthinkable otherness and separateness. But not all love between
man and woman is whole. It may be all gentle, the merging into
oneness, like St. Francis and St. Clare, or Mary of Bethany and
Jesus. There may be no separateness discovered, no singleness
won, no unique otherness admitted. This is a half love, what is
called sacred love. And this is the love which knows the purest
happiness. On the other hand, the love may be all a lovely battle
of sensual gratification, the beautiful but deadly counterposing
of male against female, as Tristan and Isolde. These are the lovers that top the sum of pride, they go with the grandest banners,
they are the gem-like beings, he pure male singled and separated
out in superb jewel-like isolation of arrogant manhood, she purely
woman, a lily balanced in rocking pride of beauty and perfume
of womanhood. This is the profane love, that ends in flamboyant
and lacerating tragedy when the two which are so singled out are
torn finally apart by death. But if profane love ends in piercing
tragedy, none the less the sacred love ends in a poignant yearn-
ing and exquisite submissive grief. St. Francis dies and leaves St.
Clare to her pure sorrow.

There must be two in one, always two in one — the sweet love
of communion and the fierce, proud love of sensual fulfilment,

both together in one love. And then we are like a rose. We sur-
pass even love, love is encompassed and surpassed. We are two
who have a pure connection. We are two, isolated like gems in
our unthinkable otherness. But the rose contains and transcends
us, we are one rose, beyond.

The Christian love, the brotherly love, this is always sacred.
I love my neighbour as myself. What then? I am enlarged, I sur-
pass myself, I become whole in mankind. In the whole of perfect
humanity I am whole. I am the microcosm, the epitome of the
great microcosm. I speak of the perfectibility of man. Man can
be made perfect in love, he can become a creature of love alone.
Then humanity shall be one whole of love. This is the perfect
future for those who love their neighbours as themselves.

But, alas! however much I may be the microcosm, the exem-
plar of brotherly love, there is in me this necessity to separate and
distinguish myself into gem-like singleness, distinct and apart from
all the rest, proud as a lion, isolated as a star. This is a necessity
within me. And this necessity is unfulfilled, it becomes stronger
and stronger and it becomes dominant.

Then I shall hate the self that I am, powerfully and profoundly
shall I hate this microcosm that I have become, this epitome of
mankind. I shall hate myself with madness the more I persist in
adhering to my achieved self of brotherly love. Still I shall persist
in representing a whole loving humanity, until the unfulfilled
passion for singleness drives me into action. Then I shall hate my
neighbour as I hate myself. And then, woe betide my neighbour and
me! Whom the gods wish to destroy they first make mad. And
this is how we become mad, by being impelled into activity by the
subconscious reaction against the self we maintain, without ever
ceasing to maintain this detested self. We are bewildered, dazed.
In the name of brotherly love we rush into stupendous blind activities of brotherly hate. We are made mad by the split, the duality
in ourselves. The gods wish to destroy us because we serve them too
well. Which is the end of brotherly love, *liberté, fraternité, égalité.*
How can there be liberty when I am not free to be other than fra-
ternal and equal? I must be free to be separate and unequal in the
finest sense, if I am to be free. *Fraternité* and *égalité,* these are
tyranny of tyrannies.

There must be brotherly love, a wholeness of humanity. But
there must also be pure, separate individuality, separate and proud
as a lion or a hawk. There must be both. In the duality lies fulfilment. Man must act in concert with man, creatively and happily.
This is greater happiness. But man must also act separately and dis-

tinctly, apart from every other man, single and self-responsible and proud with unquenchable pride, moving for himself without reference to his neighbour. These two movements are opposite, yet they do not negate each other. We have understanding. And if we understand, then we balance perfectly between the two motions, we are single, isolated individuals, we are a great concordant humanity, both, and then the rose of perfection transcends us, the rose of the world which has never yet blossomed, but which will blossom from us when we begin to understand both sides and to live in both directions, freely and without fear, following the inmost desires of our body and spirit, which arrive to us out of the unknown.

Lastly, there is the love of God; we become whole with God. But God as we know Him is either infinite love or infinite pride and power, always one or the other, Christ or Jehovah, always one half excluding the other. Therefore, God is forever jealous. If we love one God, we must hate this one sooner or later, and choose the other. This is the tragedy of religious experience. But the Holy Spirit, the unknowable, is single and perfect for us.

There is that which we cannot love, because it surpasses either love or hate. There is the unknown and the unknowable which propounds all creation. This we cannot love, we can only accept it as a term of our own limitation and ratification. We can only know that from the unknown, profound desires enter in upon us, and that the fulfilling of these desires is the fulfilling of creation. We know that the rose comes to blossom. We know that we are incipient with blossom. It is our business to go as we are impelled, with faith and pure spontaneous morality, knowing that the rose blossoms, and taking that knowledge for sufficient.

Making Love to Music

"To me, dancing," said Romeo, "is just making love to music."

"That's why you never will dance with me, I suppose," replied Juliet.

"Well, you know, you are a bit too much of an individual."

It is a curious thing, but the ideas of one generation become the instincts of the next. We are all of us, largely, the embodied ideas of our grandmothers, and, without knowing it, we behave as such. It is odd that the grafting works so quietly, but it seems to. Let the ideas change rapidly, and there follows a correspondingly rapid change in humanity. We become what we think. Worse still, we have become what our grandmothers thought. And our children's children will become the lamentable things that we are thinking. Which is the psychological visiting of the sins of the fathers upon the children. For we do not become just the lofty or beautiful thoughts of our grandmothers. Alas no! We are the embodiment of the most potent ideas of our progenitors, and these ideas are mostly private ones, not to be admitted in public, but to be transmitted as instincts and as the dynamics of behaviour to the third and fourth generation. Alas for the thing that our grandmothers brooded over in secret, and willed in private. That thing are we.

What did they wish and will? One thing is certain: they wished to be made love to, to music. They wished man were not a coarse creature, jumping to his goal, and finished. They wanted heavenly strains to resound, while he held their hand, and a new musical movement to burst forth, as he put his arm round their waist. With infinite variations the music was to soar on, from level to level of love-making, in a delicious dance, the two things inextricable, the two persons likewise.

To end, of course, before the so-called consummation of love-making, which, to our grandmothers in their dream, and therefore

39

to us in actuality, is the grand anti-climax. Not a consummation, but a humiliating anti-climax.

This is the so-called act of love itself, the actual knuckle of the whole bone of contention: a humiliating anti-climax. The bone of contention, of course, is sex. Sex is very charming and very delightful, so long as you make love to music, and you tread the clouds with Shelley, in a two-step. But to come at last to the grotesque bathos of capitulation: no sir! Nay-nay!

Even a man like Maupassant, an apparent devotee of sex, says the same thing: and Maupassant is grandfather, or great-grand-father, to very many of us. Surely, he says, the act of copulation is the Creator's cynical joke against us. To have created in us all these beautiful and noble sentiments of love, to set the nightingale and all the heavenly spheres singing, merely to throw us into this grotesque posture, to perform this humiliating act, is a piece of cynicism worthy, not of a benevolent Creator, but of a mocking demon.

Poor Maupassant, there is the clue to his own catastrophe! He wanted to make love to music. And he realized, with rage, that copulate to music you cannot. So he divided himself against himself, and damned his eyes in disgust, then copulated all the more.

We, however, his grandchildren, are shrewder. Man *must* make love to music, and woman *must* be made love to, to a string and saxophone accompaniment. It is our inner necessity. Because our grandfathers, and especially our great-grandfathers, left the music most severely out of their copulations. So now we leave the copulation most severely out of our musical love-making. We *must* make love to music: it is our grandmothers' dream, become an inward necessity in us, an unconscious motive force. Copulate you cannot, to music. So cut out that part, and solve the problem.

The popular modern dances, far from being "sexual," are distinctly anti-sexual. But there, again, we must make a distinction. We should say, the modern jazz and tango and Charleston, far from being an incitement to copulation, are in direct antagonism to copulation. Therefore it is all nonsense for the churches to raise their voice against dancing, against "making love to music." Because the Church, and society at large, has no particular antagonism to sex. It would be ridiculous, for sex is so large and all-embracing that the religious passion itself is largely sexual. But, as they say, "sublimated." This is the great recipe for sex: only sublimate it! Imagine the quicksilver heated and passing off in weird, slightly poisonous vapour, instead of heavily rolling together and fusing:

and there you have the process: sublimation: making love to music!
Morality has really no quarrel at all with "sublimated" sex. Most
"nice" things are "sublimated sex." What morality hates, what the
Church hates, what modern *mankind* hates — for what, after all, is
"morality" except the instinctive revulsion of the majority? — is just
copulation. The modern youth especially just have an instinctive
aversion from copulation. They love sex. But they inwardly loathe
copulation, even when they play at it. As for playing at it, what
else are they to do, given the toys? But they don't like it. They do
it in a sort of self-spite. And they turn away, with disgust and
relief, from this bed-ridden act, to make love once more to music.

And really, surely this is all to the good. If the young don't
really *like* copulation, then they are safe. As for marriage, they
will marry, according to their grandmothers' dream, for quite
other reasons. Our grandfathers, or great-grandfathers, married
crudely and unmusically, for copulation. That was the actuality.
So the dream was all of music. The dream was the mating of two
souls, to the faint chiming of the Seraphim. We, the third and
fourth generation, we are the dream made flesh. They dreamed
of a marriage with all things gross — meaning especially copulation — left out, and only the pure harmony of equality and inti-
mate companionship remaining. And the young live out the
dream. They marry: they copulate in a perfunctory and half-
disgusted fashion, merely to show they can do it. And so they
have children. But the marriage is made to music, the gramo-
phone and the wireless orchestrate each small domestic art, and
keep up the jazzing jig of connubial felicity, a felicity of companionship, equality, forbearance, and mutual sharing of everything the married couple have in common. Marriage set to music!
The worn-out old serpent in this musical Eden of domesticity is
the last, feeble instinct for copulation, which drives the married
couple to clash upon the boring organic differences in one another,
and prevents them from being twin souls in almost identical bodies.
But we are wise and soon learn to leave the humiliating act out
altogether. It is the only wisdom.

We are such stuff as our grandmothers' dreams were made on,
and our little life is rounded by a band.

The thing you wonder, as you watch the modern dancers making love to music, in a dance-hall, is what kind of dances will our
children's children dance? Our mothers' mothers danced quadrilles
and sets of Lancers, and the waltz was almost an indecent thing
to them. Our mothers' mothers' mothers danced minuets and

Roger de Coverleys, and smart and bouncing country dances which worked up the blood and danced a man nearer and nearer to copulation.

But lo! even while she was being whirled round in the dance, our great-grandmother was dreaming of soft and throbbing music, and the arms of "one person," and the throbbing and sliding unison of this one more elevated person, who would never coarsely bounce her towards bed and copulation, but would slide on with her forever, down the dim and sonorous vistas, making love without end to music without end, and leaving out entirely that disastrous, music-less full-stop of copulation, the end of ends.

So she dreamed, our great-grandmother, as she crossed hands and was flung around, and buffeted and busked towards bed, and the bouncing of the *bête à deux dos*. She dreamed of men that were only embodied souls, not tiresome and gross males, lords and masters. She dreamed of "one person" who was all men in one, universal, and beyond narrow individualism.

So that now, the great-granddaughter is made love to by all men — to music — as if it were one man. To music, all men, as if it were one man, make love to her, and she sways in the arms, not of an individual, but of the modern species. It is wonderful. And the modern man makes love, to music, to all women, as if she were one woman. All woman, as if she were one woman! It is almost like Baudelaire making love to the vast thighs of Dame Nature herself, except that that dream of our great-grandfather is still too copulative, though all-embracing.

But what is the dream that is simmering at the bottom of the soul of the modern young woman as she slides to music across the floor, in the arms of the species, or as she waggles opposite the species, in the Charleston? If she is content, there is no dream. But woman is never content. If she were content, the Charleston and the Black Bottom would not oust the tango.

She is not content. She is even less content, in the morning after the night before, than was her great-grandmother, who had been bounced by copulatory attentions. She is even less content; therefore her dream, though not risen yet to consciousness, is even more devouring and more rapidly subversive.

What is her dream, this slender lady just out of her teens, who is varying the two-step with the Black Bottom? What can her dream be? Because what her dream is, that her children, and my children, or children's children, will become. It is the very ovum of the future soul, as my dream is the sperm.

There is not much left for her to dream of, because whatever she wants she can have. All men, or no men, this man or that, she has the choice, for she has no lord and master. Sliding down the endless avenues of music, having an endless love endlessly made to her, she has this too. If she wants to be bounced into copulation, at a dead end, she can have that too: just to prove how monkeyish it is, and what a fumbling in the cul-de-sac.

Nothing is denied her, so there is nothing to want. And without desire, even dreams are lame. Lame dreams! Perhaps she has lame dreams, and wishes, last wish of all, she had no dreams at all.

But while life lasts, and is an affair of sleeping and waking, this is the one wish that will never be granted. From dreams no man escapeth, no woman either. Even the little blonde who is preferred by gentlemen has a dream somewhere, if she, and we, and he, did but know it. Even a dream beyond emeralds and dollars.

What is it? What is the lame and smothered dream of the lady? Whatever it is, she will never know: not till somebody has told it to her, and then gradually, and after a great deal of spiteful repudiation, she will recognize it, and it will pass into her womb.

Myself, I do not know what the frail lady's dream may be. But depend upon one thing, it will be something very different from the present business. The dream and the business! — an eternal antipathy. So the dream, whatever it may be, will *not* be "making love to music." It will be something else.

Perhaps it will be the recapturing of a dream that started in mankind, and never finished, was never fully unfolded. The thought occurred to me suddenly when I was looking at the remains of paintings on the walls of Etruscan tombs at Tarquinia. There the painted women dance, in their transparent linen with heavier coloured borders, opposite the naked-limbed men, in a splendour and an abandon which is not at all abandoned. There is a great beauty in them, as of life which has not finished. The dance is Greek, if you like, but not finished off like the Greek dancing. The beauty is not so pure, if you will, as the Greek beauty; but also it is more ample, not so narrowed. And there is not the slight element of abstraction, of inhumanity, which underlies all Greek expression, the tragic will.

The Etruscans, at least before the Romans smashed them, do not seem to have been tangled up with tragedy, as the Greeks were from the first. There seems to have been a peculiar large carelessness about them, very human and non-moral. As far as one can judge, they never said: certain acts are immoral, just because we say so! They seem to have had a strong feeling for taking life sincerely as a pleasant thing. Even death was a gay and lively affair.

Moralists will say: Divine law wiped them out. The answer to that is, divine law wipes everything out in time, even itself. And if the smashing power of the all-trampling Roman is to be identified with divine law, then all I can do is to look up another divinity.

No, I do believe that the unborn dream at the bottom of the soul of the shingled, modern young lady is this Etruscan young woman of mine, dancing with such abandon opposite her naked-limbed, strongly dancing young man, to the sound of the double flute. They are wild with a dance that is heavy and light at the same time, and not a bit anti-copulative, yet not bouncingly copulative either.

That was another nice thing about the Etruscans: there was a phallic symbol everywhere, so everybody was used to it, and they no doubt all offered it small offerings, as the source of inspiration. Being part of the everyday life, there was no need to get it on the brain, as we tend to do.

And apparently the men, the men slaves at least, went gaily and jauntily round with no clothes on at all, and, being therefore of a good brown colour, wore their skin for livery. And the Etruscan ladies thought nothing of it. Why should they? We think nothing of a naked cow, and we still refrain from putting our pet-dogs into pants or petticoats: marvellous to relate: but then, our ideal is Liberty, after all! So if the slave was stark naked, who gaily piped to the lady as she danced, and if her partner was three-parts naked, and herself nothing but a transparency, well, nobody thought anything about it; there was nothing to shy off from, and all the fun was in the dance.

There it is, the delightful quality of the Etruscan dance. They are neither making love to music, to avoid copulation, nor are they bouncing towards copulation with a brass band accompaniment. They are just dancing a dance with the elixir of life. And if they have made a little offering to the stone phallus at the door, it is because when one is full of life one is full of possibilities, and the phallus gives life. And if they have made an offering also to the queer ark of the female symbol, at the door of a woman's tomb, it is because the womb too is the source of life, and a great fountain of dance-movements.

It is we who have narrowed the dance down to two movements: either bouncing towards copulation, or sliding and shaking

and waggling, to elude it. Surely it is ridiculous to make love to
music, and to music to be made love to! Surely the music is to
dance to! And surely the modern young woman feels this, somewhere deep inside.

To the music one should dance, and dancing, dance. The
Etruscan young woman is going gaily at it, after two thousand
five hundred years. She is not making love to music, nor is the
dark-limbed youth, her partner. She is just dancing her very
soul into existence, having made an offering on one hand to the
lively phallus of man, on the other hand, to the shut womb-symbol
of woman, and put herself on real good terms with both of them.
So she is quite serene, and dancing herself as a very fountain of
motion and of life, the young man opposite her dancing himself
the same, in contrast and balance, with just the double flute to
whistle round their naked heels.

And I believe this is, or will be, the dream of our pathetic, music-
stunned young girl of today, and the substance of her children's
children, unto the third and fourth generation.

Cocksure Women and Hensure Men

It seems to me there are two aspects to women. There is the demure and the dauntless. Men have loved to dwell, in fiction at least, on the demure maiden whose inevitable reply is: Oh, yes, if you please, kind sir! The demure maiden, the demure spouse, the demure mother — this is still the ideal. A few maidens, mistresses, and mothers *are* demure. A few pretend to be. But the vast majority are not. And they don't pretend to be. We don't expect a girl skilfully driving her car to be demure, we expect her to be dauntless. What good would demure and maidenly Members of Parliament be, inevitably responding: Oh, yes, if you please, kind sir! Though of course there are masculine members of that kidney. And a demure telephone girl? Or even a demure stenographer? Demureness, to be sure, is outwardly becoming, it is an outward mark of femininity, like bobbed hair. But it goes with inward dauntlessness. The girl who has got to make her way in life has got to be dauntless, and if she has a pretty, demure manner with it, then lucky girl. She kills two birds with two stones.

With the two kinds of femininity go two kinds of confidence: there are the women who are cocksure, and the women who are hensure. A really up-to-date woman is a cocksure woman. She doesn't have a doubt nor a qualm. She is the modern type. Whereas the old-fashioned demure woman was sure as a hen is sure, that is, without knowing anything about it. She went quietly and busily clucking around, laying the eggs and mothering the chickens in a kind of anxious dream that still was full of sureness. But not mental sureness. Her sureness was a physical condition, very soothing, but a condition out of which she could easily be startled or frightened.

It is quite amusing to see the two kinds of sureness in chickens. The cockerel is, naturally, cocksure. He crows because he is *certain* it is day. Then the hen peeps out from under her wing. He marches to the door of the hen-house and pokes out his head assertively:

Ah ha! daylight, of course! just as I said! — and he majestically
steps down the chicken ladder towards *terra firma,* knowing that
the hens will step cautiously after him, drawn by his confidence.
So after him, cautiously, step the hens. He crows again: *Ha-ha!
here we are!* — It is indisputable, and the hens accept it entirely. He
marches towards the house. From the house a person ought to appear, scattering corn. Why does the person not appear? The cock
will see to it. He is cocksure. He gives a loud crow in the doorway,
and the person appears. The hens are suitably impressed, but immediately devote all their henny consciousness to the scattered corn,
pecking absorbedly, while the cock runs and fusses, cocksure that
he is responsible for it all.

So the day goes on. The cock finds a tit-bit, and loudly calls
the hens. They scuffle up in henny surety, and gobble the tit-bit.
But when they find a juicy morsel for themselves, they devour it
in silence, hensure. Unless, of course, there are little chicks, when
they most anxiously call the brood. But in her own dim surety,
the hen is really much surer than the cock, in a different way.
She marches off to lay her egg, she secures obstinately the nest she
wants, she lays her egg at last, then steps forth again with pranc-
ing confidence, and gives that most assured of all sounds, the hensure cackle of a bird who has laid her egg. The cock, who is never
so sure about anything as the hen is about the egg she has laid,
immediately starts to cackle like the female of his species. He is
pining to be hensure, for hensure is so much surer than cocksure.

Nevertheless, cocksure is boss. When the chicken-hawk appears
in the sky, loud are the cockerel's calls of alarm. Then the hens
scuffle under the veranda, the cock ruffles his feathers on guard.
The hens are numb with fear, they say: Alas, there is no health
in us! How wonderful to be a cock so bold! And they huddle,
numbed. But their very numbness is hensurety.

Just as the cock can cackle, however, as if he had laid the egg,
so can the hen bird crow. She can more or less assume his cocksureness. And yet she is never so easy, cocksure, as she used to be
when she was hensure. Cocksure, she is cocksure, but uneasy. Hensure, she trembles, but is easy.

It seems to me just the same in the vast human farmyard.
Only nowadays all the cocks are cackling and pretending to lay
eggs, and all the hens are crowing and pretending to call the
sun out of bed. If women today are cocksure, men are hensure.
Men are timid, tremulous, rather soft and submissive, easy in
their very henlike tremulousness. They only want to be spoken

to gently. So the women step forth with a good loud *cock-a-doodle-do!*

The tragedy about cocksure women is that they are more cocky, in their assurance, than the cock himself. They never realize that when the cock gives his loud crow in the morning, he listens acutely afterwards, to hear if some other wretch of a cock dare crow defiance, challenge. To the cock, there is always defiance, challenge, danger, and death on the clear air; or the possibility thereof.

But alas, when the hen crows, she listens for no defiance or challenge. When she says *cock-a-doodle-do!* then it is unanswerable. The cock listens for an answer, alert. But the hen knows she is unanswerable. *Cock-a-doodle-do!* and their it is, take it or leave it!

And it is this that makes the cocksureness of women so dangerous, so devastating. It is really out of scheme, it is not in relation to the rest of things. So we have the tragedy of cocksure women. They find, so often, that instead of having laid an egg they have laid a vote, or an empty ink-bottle, or some other absolutely unhatchable object, which means nothing to them.

It is the tragedy of the modern woman. She becomes cocksure, she puts all her passion and energy and years of her life into some effort or assertion, without ever listening for the denial which she ought to take into count. She is cocksure, but she is a hen all the time. Frightened of her own henny self, she rushes to mad lengths about votes, or welfare, or sports, or business: she is marvellous, out-manning the man. But alas, it is all fundamentally disconnected. It is all an attitude, and one day the attitude will become a weird cramp, a pain, and then it will collapse. And when it has collapsed, and she looks at the eggs she has laid, votes, or miles of typewriting, years of business efficiency — suddenly, because she is a hen and not a cock, all she has done will turn into pure nothingness to her. Suddenly it all falls out of relation to her basic henny self, and she realizes she has lost her life. The lovely henny surety, the hensureness which is the real bliss of every female, has been denied her: she had never had it. Having lived her life with such utmost strenuousness and cocksureness, she has missed her life altogether. Nothingness!

Sex versus Loveliness

It is a pity that *sex* is such an ugly little word. An ugly little word, and really almost incomprehensible. What *is* sex, after all? The more we think about it the less we know.

Science says it is an instinct; but what is an instinct? Apparently an instinct is an old, old habit that has become ingrained. But a habit, however old, has to have a beginning. And there is really no beginning to sex. Where life is, there it is. So sex is no "habit" that has been formed.

Again, they talk of sex as an appetite, like hunger. An appetite; but for what? An appetite for propagation? It is rather absurd. They say a peacock puts on all his fine feathers to dazzle the peahen into letting him satisfy his appetite for propagation. But why should the peahen not put on fine feathers, to dazzle the peacock, and satisfy *her* desire for propagation? She has surely quite as great a desire for eggs and chickens as he has. We cannot believe that her sex urge is so weak that she needs all that blue splendour of feathers to rouse her. Not at all.

As for me, I never even saw a peahen so much as look at her lord's bronze and blue glory. I don't believe she ever sees it. I don't believe for a moment that she knows the difference between bronze, blue, brown, or green.

If I had ever seen a peahen gazing with rapt attention on her lord's flamboyancy, I might believe that he had put on all those feathers just to "attract" her. But she never looks at him. Only she seems to get a little perky when he shudders all his quills at her, like a storm in the trees. Then she does seem to notice, just casually, his presence.

These theories of sex are amazing. A peacock puts on his glory for the sake of a wall-eyed peahen who never looks at him. Imagine a scientist being so naïve as to credit the peahen with a profound, dynamic appreciation of a peacock's colour and pattern. Oh, highly aesthetic peahen!

And a nightingale sings to attract his female. Which is mighty curious, seeing he sings his best when courtship and honeymoon are over and the female is no longer concerned with him at all, but with the young. Well, then, if he doesn't sing to attract her, he must sing to distract her and amuse her while she's sitting.

How delightful, how naïve theories are! But there is a hidden will behind them all. There is a hidden will behind all theories of sex, implacable. And that is the will to deny, to wipe out the mystery of beauty.

Because beauty is a mystery. You can neither eat it nor make flannel out of it. Well, then, says science, it is just a trick to catch the female and induce her to propagate. How naïve! As if the female needed inducing. She will propagate in the dark, even — so where, then, is the beauty trick?

Science has a mysterious hatred of beauty, because it doesn't fit in the cause-and-effect chain. And society has a mysterious hatred of sex, because it perpetually interferes with the nice money-making schemes of social man. So the two hatreds made a combine, and sex and beauty are mere propagation appetite.

Now sex and beauty are one thing, like flame and fire. If you hate sex you hate beauty. If you love *living* beauty, you have a reverence for sex. Of course you can love old, dead beauty and hate sex. But to love living beauty you must have a reverence for sex.

Sex and beauty are inseparable, like life and consciousness. And the intelligence which goes with sex and beauty, and arises out of sex and beauty, is intuition. The great disaster of our civilization is the morbid hatred of sex. What, for example, could show a more poisoned hatred of sex than Freudian psychoanalysis? — which carries with it a morbid fear of beauty, "alive" beauty, and which causes the atrophy of our intuitive faculty and our intuitive self.

The deep psychic disease of modern men and women is the diseased, atrophied condition of the intuitive faculties. There is a whole world of life that we might know and enjoy by intuition, and by intuition alone. This is denied us, because we deny sex and beauty, the source of the intuitive life and of the insouciance which is so lovely in free animals and in plants.

Sex is the root of which intuition is the foliage and beauty the flower. Why is a woman lovely, if ever, in her twenties? It is the time when sex rises softly to her face, as a rose to the top of a rose bush.

And the appeal is the appeal of beauty. We deny it wherever we can. We try to make the beauty as shallow and trashy as possible. But, first and foremost, sex appeal is the appeal of beauty.

Now beauty is a thing about which we are so uneducated we can hardly speak of it. We try to pretend it is a fixed arrangement: straight nose, large eyes, etc. We think a lovely woman must look like Lillian Gish, a handsome man must look like Rudolph Valentino. Se we *think*.

In actual life we behave quite differently. We say "She's quite beautiful, but I don't care for her." Which shows we are using the word *beautiful* all wrong. We should say: "She has the stereotyped attributes of beauty, but she is not beautiful to me."

Beauty is an *experience,* nothing else. It is not a fixed pattern or an arrangement of features. It is something *felt,* a glow or a communicated sense of fineness. What ails us is that our sense of beauty is so bruised and blunted, we miss all the best.

But to stick to the films — there is a greater essential beauty in Charlie Chaplin's odd face than ever there was in Valentino's. There is a bit of true beauty in Chaplin's brows and eyes, a gleam of something pure.

But our sense of beauty is so bruised and clumsy, we don't see it, and don't know it when we do see it. We can only see the blatantly obvious, like the so-called beauty of Rudolph Valentino, which only pleases because it satisfies some ready-made notion of handsomeness.

But the plainest person can look beautiful, can *be* beautiful. It only needs the fire of sex to rise delicately to change an ugly face to a lovely one. That is really sex appeal: the communicating of a sense of beauty.

And in the reverse way, no one can be quite so repellent as a really pretty woman. That is, since beauty is a question of experience, not of concrete form, no one can be as acutely ugly as a really pretty woman. When the sex glow is missing, and she moves in ugly coldness, how hideous she seems, and all the worse for her externals of prettiness.

What sex is, we don't know, but it must be some sort of fire. For it always communicates a sense of warmth, of glow. And when the glow becomes a pure shine, then we feel the sense of beauty.

But the communicating of the warmth, the glow of sex, is true sex appeal. We all have the fire of sex slumbering or burning inside us. If we live to be ninety, it is still there. Or, if it dies, we become one of those ghastly living corpses which are unfortunately becoming more numerous in the world.

Nothing is more ugly than a human being in whom the fire of sex has gone out. You get a nasty clayey creature whom everybody wants to avoid.

But while we are fully alive, the fire of sex smoulders or burns in us. In youth it flickers and shines; in age it glows softer and stiller, but there it is. We have some control over it; but only partial control. That is why society hates it.

While ever it lives, the fire of sex, which is the source of beauty and anger, burns in us beyond our understanding. Like actual fire, while it lives it will burn our fingers if we touch it carelessly. And so social man, who only wants to be "safe," hates the fire of sex.

Luckily, not many men succeed in being merely social men. The fire of the old Adam smoulders. And one of the qualities of fire is that it calls to fire. Sex-fire here kindles sex-fire there. It may only rouse the smoulder into a soft glow. It may call up a sharp flicker. Or rouse a flame; and then flame leans to flame, and starts a blaze.

Whenever the sex-fire glows through, it will kindle an answer somewhere or other. It may only kindle a sense of warmth and optimism. Then you say: "I like that girl; she's a real good sort." It may kindle a glow that makes the world look kindlier, and life feel better. Then you say: "She's an attractive woman. I like her."

Or she may rouse a flame that lights up her own face first, before it lights up the universe. Then you say: "She's a lovely woman. She looks lovely to me."

It takes a rare woman to rouse a real sense of loveliness. It is not that a woman is born beautiful. We say that to escape our own poor, bruised, clumsy understanding of beauty. There have been thousands and thousands of women quite as good-looking as Diane de Poitiers, or Mrs. Langtry, or any of the famous ones. There are today thousands and thousands of superbly good-looking women. But oh, how few lovely women!

And why? Because of the failure of their sex appeal. A good-looking woman becomes lovely when the fire of sex rouses pure and fine in her and flickers through her face and touches the fire in me.

Then she becomes a lovely woman to me, then she is in the living flesh a lovely woman: not a mere photograph of one. And how lovely a lovely woman! But, alas! how rare! How bitterly rare in a world full of unusually handsome girls and women!

Handsome, good-looking, but not lovely, not beautiful. Handsome and good-looking women are the women with good features and the right hair. But a lovely woman is an experience. It is a question of communicated fire. It is a question of sex appeal in our poor, dilapidated modern phraseology. Sex appeal applied to Diane de Poitiers, or even, in the lovely hours, to one's wife — why, it is a libel and a slander in itself. Nowadays, however, instead of the fire of loveliness, it is sex appeal. The two are the same thing, I suppose, but on vastly different levels.

The business man's pretty and devoted secretary is still chiefly valuable because of her sex appeal. Which does not imply "immoral relations" in the slightest.

Even today a girl with a bit of generosity likes to feel she is helping a man if the man will take her help. And this desire that he shall take her help is her sex appeal. It is the genuine fire, if of a very mediocre heat.

Still, it serves to keep the world of "business" alive. Probably, but for the introduction of the lady secretary into the business man's office, the business man would have collapsed entirely by now. She calls up the sacred fire in her and she communicates it to her boss. He feels an added flow of energy and optimism, and — business flourishes.

There is, of course, the other side of sex appeal. It can be the destruction of the one appealed to. When a woman starts using her sex appeal to her own advantage it is usually a bad moment for some poor devil. But this side of sex appeal has been overworked lately, so it is not nearly as dangerous as it was.

The sex-appealing courtesans who ruined so many men in Balzac no longer find it smooth running. Men have grown canny. They fight shy even of the emotional vamp. In fact, men are inclined to think they smell a rat the moment they feel the touch of feminine sex appeal today.

Which is a pity, for sex appeal is only a dirty name for a bit of life-flame. No man works so well and so successfully as when some woman has kindled a little fire in his veins. No woman does her housework with real joy unless she is in love — and a woman may go on being quietly in love for fifty years almost without knowing it.

If only our civilization had taught us how to let sex appeal flow properly and subtly, how to keep the fire of sex clear and alive, flickering or glowing or blazing in all its varying degrees of strength and communication, we might, all of us, have lived all our lives in love, which means we should be kindled and full of zest in all kinds of ways and for all kinds of things. . . .

Whereas, what a lot of dead ash there is in life now.

Introduction to *Pansies*

(Unexpurgated Edition)

This little bunch of fragments is offered as a bunch of *pensées,*
anglicé pansies; a handful of thoughts. Or, if you will have the
other derivation of pansy, from *panser,* to dress or soothe a wound,
these are my tender administrations to the mental and emotional
wounds we suffer from. Or you can have heartsease if you like,
since the modern heart could certainly do with it.

Each little piece is a thought; not a bare idea or an opinion
or a didactic statement, but a true thought, which comes as much
from the heart and the genitals as from the head. A thought, with
its own blood of emotion and instinct running in it like the fire
in a fire-opal, if I may be so bold. Perhaps if you hold up my pansies properly to the light, they may show a running vein of fire.
At least, they do not pretend to be half-baked lyrics or melodies
in American measure. They are thoughts which run through the
modern mind and body, each having its own separate existence,
yet each of them combining with all the others to make up a
complete state of mind.

It suits the modern temper better to have its state of mind
made up of apparently irrelevant thoughts that scurry in different
directions, yet belong to the same nest; each thought trotting
down the page like an independent creature, each with its own
small head and tail, trotting its own little way, then curling up
to sleep. We prefer it, at least the young seem to prefer it to those
solid blocks of mental pabulum packed like bales in the pages of
a proper heavy book. Even we prefer it to those slightly didactic
opinions and slices of wisdom which are laid horizontally across
the pages of Pascal's *Pensées* or La Bruyère's *Caractères,* separated
only by *pattes de mouches,* like faint sprigs of parsley. Let every
pensée trot on its own little paws, not be laid like a cutlet trimmed
with a *patte de mouche.*

Live and let live, and each pansy will tip you its separate wink.
The fairest thing in nature, a flower, still has its roots in earth and

manure; and in the perfume there hovers still the faint strange scent of earth, the under-earth in all its heavy humidity and darkness. Certainly it is so in pansy-scent, and in violet-scent; mingled with the blue of the morning the black of the corrosive humus. Else the scent would be just sickly sweet.

So it is: we all have our roots in earth. And it is our roots that now need a little attention, need the hard soil eased away from them, and softened so that a little fresh air can come to them, and they can breathe. For by pretending to have no roots, we have trodden the earth so hard over them that they are starving and stifling below the soil. We have roots, and our roots are in the sensual, instinctive and intuitive body, and it is here we need fresh air of open consciousness.

I am abused most of all for using the so-called "obscene" words. Nobody quite knows what the word "obscene" itself means, or what it is intended to mean: but gradually all the *old* words that belong to the body below the navel have come to be judged obscene. Obscene means today that the policeman thinks he has a right to arrest you, nothing else.

Myself, I am mystified at this horror over a mere word, a plain simple word that stands for a plain simple thing. "In the beginning was the Word, and the Word was God and the Word was with God." If that is true, then we are very far from the beginning. When did the Word "fall"? When did the Word become unclean "below the navel"? Because today, if you suggest that the word *arse* was in the beginning and was God and was with God, you will just be put in prison at once. Though a doctor might say the same of the word *ischial tuberosity,* and all the old ladies would piously murmur "Quite!" Now that sort of thing is idiotic and humiliating. Whoever the God was that made us, He made us complete. He didn't stop at the navel and leave the rest to the devil. It is too childish. And the same with the Word which is God. If the Word is God — which in the sense of the human it is — then you can't suddenly say that all the words which belong below the navel are obscene. The word arse is as much god as the word face. It must be so, otherwise you cut off your god at the waist.

What is obvious is that the words in these cases have been dirtied by the mind, by unclean mental associations. The words themselves are clean, so are the things to which they apply. But the mind drags in a filthy association, calls up some repulsive emotion. Well, then, cleanse the mind, that is the real job. It is the mind which is the Augean stables, not language. The word arse is clean enough. Even the part of the body it refers to is just as much me as my hand and my brain are me. It is not for *me* to quarrel with my own natural make-up. If I am, I am all that I am. But the impudent and dirty mind won't have it. It hates certain parts of the body, and makes the words representing these parts scapegoats. It pelts them out of the consciousness with filth, and there they hover, never dying, never dead, slipping into the consciousness again unawares, and pelted out again with filth, haunting the margins of the consciousness like jackals or hyenas. And they refer to parts of our own living bodies, and to our most essential acts. So that man turns himself into a thing of shame and horror. And his consciousness shudders with horrors that he has made for himself.

That sort of thing has got to stop. We can't have the consciousness haunted any longer by repulsive spectres which are no more than poor simple scapegoat words representing parts of man himself; words that the cowardly and unclean mind has driven out into the limbo of the unconscious, whence they return upon us looming and magnified out of all proportion, frightening us beyond all reasons. We must put an end to that. It is the self divided against itself most dangerously. The simple and natural "obscene" words must be cleaned up of all their depraved fear-association, and readmitted into the consciousness to take their natural place. Now they are magnified out of all proportion, so is the mental fear they represent. We must accept the word arse as we accept the word face, since arses we have and always shall have. We can't start cutting off the buttocks of unfortunate mankind, like the ladies in the Voltaire story, just to fit the mental expulsion of the word.

This scapegoat business does the mind itself so much damage. There is a poem of Swift's which should make us pause. It is written to Celia, his Celia — and every verse ends with the mad, maddened refrain: "But — Celia, Celia, Celia shits!" Now that, stated baldly, is so ridiculous it is almost funny. But when one remembers the gnashing insanity to which the great mind of Swift was reduced by that and similar thoughts, the joke dies away. Such thoughts poisoned him, like some terrible constipation. They poisoned his mind. And why, in heaven's name? The *fact* cannot have troubled him, since it applied to himself and to all of us. It was not the fact that Celia shits which so deranged him, it was the *thought*. His mind couldn't bear the thought. Great wit as he was, he could not see how ridiculous his revulsions were. His arrogant mind overbore him. He couldn't even see how much worse it would be if Celia didn't shit. His physical sympathies were too weak, his guts were too cold to sympathize with poor Celia in her natural functions. His insolent and sicklily squeamish mind just turned her into a thing of horror, because she was merely natural and went to the w.c. It is monstrous! One feels like going back across all the years to poor Celia, to say to her: It's all right, don't you take any notice of that mental lunatic.

And Swift's form of madness is very common today. Men with cold guts and over-squeamish minds are always thinking those things and squirming. Wretched man is the victim of his own little revulsions, which he magnifies into great horrors and terrifying taboos. We are all savages, we all have taboos. The Australian black may have the kangaroo for his taboo. And then he will probably die of shock and terror if a kangaroo happens to touch him. Which is what I would call a purely unnecessary death. But modern men have even more dangerous taboos. To us, certain words, certain ideas are taboo, and if they come upon us and we can't drive them away, we die or go mad with a degraded sort of terror. Which is what happened to Swift. He was such a great wit. And the modern mind altogether is falling into this form of degraded taboo-insanity. I call it a waste of sane human consciousness. But it is very dangerous, dangerous to the individual and utterly dangerous to society as a whole. Nothing is so fearful in a mass civilization like ours as a mass insanity.

The remedy is, of course, the same in both cases: lift off the taboo. The kangaroo is a harmless animal, the word shit is a harmless word. Make either into a taboo, and it becomes more dangerous. The result of taboo is insanity. And insanity, especially mob insanity, mass insanity, is the fearful danger that threatens our civilization. There are certain persons with a sort of rabies, who live only to infect the mass. If the young do not watch out, they will find themselves, before so very many years are past, engulfed in a howling manifestation of mob insanity, truly terrifying to think of. It will be better to be dead than to live to see it. Sanity, wholeness, is everything. In the name of piety and purity, what a mass of disgusting insanity is spoken and written. We shall have to fight the mob, in order to keep sane, and to keep society sane.

The State of Funk

What is the matter with the English, that they are so scared of everything? They are in a state of blue funk, and they behave like a lot of mice when somebody stamps on the floor. They are terrified about money, finance, about ships, about war, about work, about Labour, about Bolshevism, and, funniest of all, they are scared stiff of the printed word. Now this is a very strange and humiliating state of mind, in a people which has always been so dauntless. And for the nation, it is a very dangerous state of mind. When a people falls into a state of funk, then God help it. Because mass funk leads some time or other to mass panic, and then — one can only repeat, God help us.

There is, of course, a certain excuse for fear. The time of change is upon us. The need for change has taken hold of us. We are changing, we have got to change, and we can no more help it than leaves can help going yellow and coming loose in autumn, or than bulbs can help shoving their little green spikes out of the ground in spring. We are changing, we are in the throes of change, and the change will be a great one. Instinctively, we feel it. Intuitively, we know it. And we are frightened. Because change hurts. And also, in the periods of serious transition, everything is uncertain, and living things are most vulnerable.

But what of it? Granted all the pains and dangers and uncertainties, there is no excuse for falling into a state of funk. If we come to think of it, every child that is begotten and born is a seed of change, a danger to its mother, at childbirth a great pain, and, after birth, a new responsibility, a new change. If we feel in a state of funk about it, we should cease having children altogether. *If* we fall into a state of funk, indeed, the best thing is to have no children. But why fall into a state of funk?

Why not look things in the face like men, and like women? A woman who is going to have a child says to herself: Yes, I feel uncomfortable, sometimes I feel wretched, and I have a time of pain and danger ahead of me. But I have a good chance of coming through all right, especially if I am intelligent, and I bring a new life into the world. Somewhere I feel hopeful, even happy. So I must take the sour with the sweet. There is no birth without birth pangs.

It is the business of men, of course, to take the same attitude towards the birth of new conditions, new ideas, new emotions. And sorry to say, most modern men don't. They fall into a state of funk. We all of us know that ahead of us lies a great social change, a great social readjustment. A few men look it in the face and try to realize what will be best. We none of us *know* what will be best. There is no ready-made solution. Ready-made solutions are almost the greatest danger of all. A change is a slow flux, which must happen bit by bit. And it must *happen*. You can't drive it like a steam engine. But all the time you can be alert and intelligent about it, and watch for the next step, and watch for the direction of the main trend. Patience, alertness, intelligence, and a human good will and fearlessness, that is what you want in a time of change. Not funk.

Now England is on the brink of great changes, radical changes. Within the next fifty years the whole framework of our social life will be altered, will be greatly modified. The old world of our grandfathers is disappearing like thawing snow, and is as likely to cause a flood. What the world of our grandchildren will be, fifty years hence, we don't know. But in its social form it will be very different from our world of today. We've got to change. And in our power to change, in our capacity to make new intelligent adaptation to new conditions, in our readiness to admit and fulfill new needs, to give expression to new desires and new feelings, lies our hope and our health. Courage is the great word. Funk spells sheer disaster.

There is a great change coming, bound to come. The whole money arrangement will undergo a change: what, I don't know. The whole industrial system will undergo a change. Work will be different and pay will be different. The owning of property will be different. Class will be different, and human relations will be modified and perhaps simplified. If we are intelligent, alert, and undaunted, then life will be much better, more generous, more spontaneous, more vital, less basely materialistic. If we fall into a state of funk, impotence, and persecution, then things may be very much worse than they are now. It is up to us. It is up to men to be men. While men are courageous and willing to change, nothing terribly bad can happen. But once men fall into a state of funk, with the inevitable accompaniment of bullying and repression, then only bad things can happen. To be firm is one thing. But bullying is another. And bullying of any sort whatsoever can have nothing but disastrous results. And when the mass falls into a state of funk, and you have mass bullying, then catastrophe is near.

Change in the whole social system is inevitable not merely because conditions change — though partly for that reason — but because people themselves change. We change, you and I, we change and change vitally, as the years go on. New feelings arise in us, old values depreciate, new values arise. Things we thought we wanted most intensely we realize we don't care about. The things we built our lives on crumble and disappear, and the process is painful. But it is not tragic. A tadpole that has so gaily waved its tail in the water must feel very sick when the tail begins to drop off and little legs begin to sprout. The tail was its dearest, gayest, most active member, all its little life was in its tail. And now the tail must go. It seems rough on the tadpole; but the little green frog in the grass is a new gem, after all.

As a novelist, I feel it is the change inside the individual which is my real concern. The great social change interests me and troubles me, but it is not my field. I know a change is coming — and I know we must have a more generous, more human system based on the life values and not on the money values. That I know. But what steps to take I don't know. Other men know better.

My field is to know the feelings inside a man, and to make new feelings conscious. What really torments civilized people is that they are full of feelings they know nothing about; they can't realize them, they can't fulfil them, they can't *live* them. And so they are tortured. It is like having energy you can't use — it destroys you. And feelings are a form of vital energy.

I am convinced that the majority of people today have good, generous feelings which they can never know, never experience, because of some fear, some repression. I do not believe that people would be villains, thieves, murderers, and sexual criminals if they were freed from legal restraint. On the contrary, I think the vast majority would be much more generous, good-hearted, and decent if they felt they dared be. I am convinced that people want to be more decent, more good-hearted than our social system of money and grab allows them to be. The awful fight for money, into which we are all forced, hurts our good nature more than we can bear. I am sure this is true of a vast number of people.

And the same is true of our sexual feelings; only worse. There, we start all wrong. Consciously, there is supposed to be no such thing as sex in the human being. As far as possible, we never speak of it, never mention it, never, if we can help it, even think of it. It is disturbing. It is — somehow — wrong.

The whole trouble with sex is that we daren't speak of it and think of it naturally. We are not secretly sexual villains. We are not secretly sexually depraved. We are just human beings with living sex. We are all right, if we had not this unaccountable and disastrous *fear* of sex. I know, when I was a lad of eighteen, I used to remember with shame and rage in the morning the sexual thoughts and desires I had had the night before. Shame, and rage, and terror lest anybody else should have to know. And I *hated* the self that I had been, the night before.

Most boys are like that, and it is, of course, utterly wrong. The boy that had excited sexual thoughts and feelings was the living, warm-hearted, passionate me. The boy that in the morning remembered these feelings with such fear, shame and rage was the social mental me: perhaps a little priggish, and certainly in a state of funk. But the two were divided against one another. A boy divided against himself; a girl divided against herself; a people divided against itself; it is a disastrous condition.

And it was a long time before I was able to say to myself: I am *not* going to be ashamed of my sexual thoughts and desires, they are me myself, they are part of my life. I am going to accept myself sexually as I accept myself mentally and spiritually, and know that I am one time one thing, one time another, but I am always myself. My sex is me as my mind is me, and nobody will make me feel shame about it.

It is long since I came to that decision. But I remember how much freer I felt, how much warmer and more sympathetic towards people. I had no longer anything to hide from them, no longer anything to be in a funk about, lest they should find it out. My sex was me, like my mind and my spirit. And the other man's sex was him, as his mind was him, and his spirit was him. And the woman's sex was her, as her mind and spirit were herself too. And once this quiet admission is made, it is wonderful how much deeper and more real the human sympathy flows. And it is wonderful how difficult the admission is to make, for man or woman: the tacit, natural admission, that allows the natural warm flow of the blood sympathy, without repression and holding back.

I remember when I was a very young man I was enraged when with a woman, if I was reminded of her sexual actuality. I only wanted to be aware of her personality, her mind and spirit. The other had to be fiercely shut out. Some part of the natural sympathy for a woman had to be shut away, cut off. There was a mutilation in the relationship all the time.

Now, in spite of the hostility of society, I have learned a little better. Now I know that a woman is her sexual self too, and I can feel the normal sex sympathy with her. And this silent sympathy is utterly different from desire or anything rampant or lurid. If I can really sympathize with a woman in her sexual self, it is just a form of warm-heartedness and compassionateness, the most natural life-flow in the world. And it may be a woman of seventy-five, or a child of two, it is the same. But our civilization, with its horrible fear and funk and repression and bullying, has almost destroyed the natural flow of common sympathy between men and men, and men and women.

And it is this that I want to restore into life: just the natural warm flow of common sympathy between man and man, man and woman. Many people hate it, of course. Many men hate it that one should tacitly take them for sexual, physical men instead of mere social and mental personalities. Many women hate it the same. Some, the worst, are in a state of rabid funk. The papers call me "lurid" and a "dirty-minded fellow." One woman, evidently a woman of education and means, wrote to me out of the blue: "You, who are a mixture of the missing link and the chimpanzee, etc." — and told me my name stank in men's nostrils: though, since she was Mrs. Something or other, she might have said women's nostrils. And these people think they are being perfectly well-bred and perfectly "right." They are safe inside the convention, which also agrees that we are sexless creatures and social beings merely, cold and bossy and assertive, cowards safe inside a convention.

Now I am one of the least lurid mortals, and I don't at all mind being likened to a chimpanzee. If there is one thing I don't like it is cheap and promiscuous sex. If there is one thing I insist on it is that sex is a delicate, vulnerable, vital thing that you mustn't fool with. If there is one thing I deplore it is heartless sex. Sex must be a real flow, a real flow of sympathy, generous and warm, and not a trick thing, or a moment's excitation, or a mere bit of bullying.

And if I write a book about the sex relations of a man and a woman, it is not because I want all men and women to begin having indiscriminate lovers and love affairs, off the reel. All this horrid scramble of love affairs and prostitution is only part of the funk, bravado, and *doing it on purpose*. And bravado and *doing it on purpose* is just as unpleasant and hurtful as repression, just as much a sign of secret fear.

What you have to do is to get out of the state of funk, sex funk. And to do so, you've got to be perfectly decent, and you have to accept sex fully in the consciousness. Accept sex in the consciousness, and let the normal physical awareness come back, between you and other people. Be tacitly and simply aware of the sexual being in every man and woman, child and animal; and unless the man or woman is a bully, be sympathetically aware. It is the most important thing just now, this gentle physical awareness. It keeps us tender and alive at a moment when the great danger is to go brittle, hard, and in some way dead.

Accept the sexual, physical being of yourself, and of every other creature. Don't be afraid of it. Don't be afraid of the physical functions. Don't be afraid of the so-called obscene words. There is nothing wrong with the words. It is your fear that makes them bad, your needless fear. It is your fear which cuts you off physically even from your nearest and dearest. And when men and women are physically cut off, they become at last dangerous, bullying, cruel. Conquer the fear of sex, and restore the natural flow. Restore even the so-called obscene words, which are part of the natural flow. If you don't, if you don't put back a bit of the old warmth into life, there is savage disaster ahead.

Pornography and Obscenity

~~~~~~

What they are depends, as usual, entirely on the individual. What is pornography to one man is the laughter of genius to another.

The word itself, we are told, means "pertaining to harlots" — the graph of the harlot. But nowadays, what is a harlot? If she was a woman who took money from a man in return for going to bed with him — really, most wives sold themselves, in the past, and plenty of harlots gave themselves, when they felt like it, for nothing. If a woman hasn't got a tiny streak of a harlot in her, she's a dry stick as a rule. And probably most harlots had somewhere a streak of womanly generosity. Why be so cut and dried? The law is a dreary thing, and its judgments have nothing to do with life.

The same with the word "obscene": nobody knows what it means. Suppose it were derived from *obscena:* that which might not be represented on the stage; how much further are you? None! What is obscene to Tom is not obscene to Lucy or Joe, and really, the meaning of a word has to wait for majorities to decide it. If a play shocks ten people in an audience, and doesn't shock the remaining five hundred, then it is obscene to ten and innocuous to five hundred; hence the play is not obscene, by majority. But *Hamlet* shocked all the Cromwellian Puritans, and shocks nobody today, and some of Aristophanes shocks everybody today, and didn't galvanize the later Greeks at all, apparently. Man is a changeable beast, and words change their meanings with him, and things are not what they seemed, and what's what becomes what isn't, and if we think we know where we are it's only because we are so rapidly being translated to somewhere else. We have to leave everything to the majority, everything to the majority, everything to the mob, the mob, the mob. They know what is obscene and what isn't, they do. If the lower ten million doesn't know better than the upper ten men, then there's something wrong with mathematics. Take a vote on it! Show hands, and prove it by count! *Vox populi, vox Dei. Odi profanum vulgus! Profanum vulgus.*

So it comes down to this: if you are talking to the mob, the meaning of your words is the mob-meaning, decided by majority. As somebody wrote to me: the American law on obscenity is very plain, and America is going to enforce the law. Quite, my dear, quite, quite, quite! The mob knows all about obscenity. Mild little words that rhyme with spit or farce are the height of obscenity. Supposing a printer put "h" in the place of "p," by mistake, in that mere word spit? Then the great American public knows that this man has committed an obscenity, an indecency, that his act was lewd, and as a compositor he was pornographical. You can't tamper with the great public, British or American. *Vox populi, vox Dei,* don't you know. If you don't we'll let you know it. At the same time, this *vox Dei* shouts with praise over moving-pictures and books and newspaper accounts that seem, to a sinful nature like mine, completely disgusting and obscene. Like a real prude and Puritan, I have to look the other way. When obscenity becomes mawkish, which is its palatable form for the public, and when the *Vox populi, vox Dei,* is hoarse with sentimental indecency, then I have to steer away, like a Pharisee, afraid of being contaminated. There is a certain kind of sticky universal pitch that I refuse to touch.

So again, it comes down to this: you accept the majority, the mob, and its decisions, or you don't. You bow down before the *Vox populi, vox Dei,* or you plug your ears not to hear its obscene howl. You perform your antics to please the vast public, *Deus ex machina,* or you refuse to perform for the public at all, unless now and then to pull its elephantine and ignominious leg.

When it comes to the meaning of anything, even the simplest word, then you must pause. Because there are two great categories of meaning, forever separate. There is mob-meaning, and there is individual meaning. Take even the word "bread." The mob-meaning is merely: stuff made with white flour into loaves that you eat. But take the individual meaning of the word bread: the white, the brown, the corn-pone, the homemade, the smell of bread just out of the oven, the crust, the crumb, the unleavened bread, the shew-bread, the staff of life, sour-dough bread, cottage loaves, French bread, Viennese bread, black bread, a yesterday's loaf, rye, Graham, barley, rolls, *Bretzeln, Kringeln,* scones, damper, matsen — there is no end to it all, and the word bread will take you to the ends of time and space, and far-off down avenues of memory. But this is individual. The word bread will take the individual off on his own journey, and its meaning will be his own meaning, based on his own genuine imaginative reactions. And when a word comes to us in its individual character, and starts in us the individual responses, it is a great pleasure to us. The American advertisers have discovered this, and some of the cunningest American literature is to be found in advertisements of soap-suds, for example. These advertisements are *almost* prose-poems. They give the word soap-suds a bubbly, shiny individual meaning, which is very skilfully poetic, would, perhaps, be quite poetic to the mind which could forget that the poetry was bait on a hook.

Business is discovering the individual, dynamic meaning of words, and poetry is losing it. Poetry more and more tends to farfetch its word-meanings, and this results once again in mob-meanings, which arouse only a mob-reaction in the individual. For every man has a mob-self and an individual self, in varying proportions. Some men are almost all mob-self, incapable of imaginative individual responses. The worst specimens of mob-self are usually to be found in the professions, lawyers, professors, clergymen, and so on. The business man, much maligned, has a tough outside mob-self, and a scared, floundering, yet still alive individual self. The public, which is feeble-minded like an idiot, will never be able to preserve its individual reactions from the tricks of the exploiter. The public is always exploited and always will be exploited. The methods of exploitation merely vary. Today the public is tickled into laying the golden egg. With imaginative words and individual meanings it is tricked into giving the great goose-cackle of mob-acquiescence. *Vox populi, vox Dei.* It has always been so, and will always be so. Why? Because the public has not enough wit to distinguish between mob-meanings and individual meanings. The mass is forever vulgar, because it can't distinguish between its own original feelings and feelings which are diddled into existence by the exploiter. The public is always profane, because it is controlled from the outside, by the trickster, and never from the inside, by its own sincerity. The mob is always obscene, because it is always second-hand.

Which brings us back to our subject of pornography and obscenity. The reaction to any word may be, in any individual, either a mob-reaction or an individual reaction. It is up to the individual to ask himself: Is my reaction individual, or am I merely reacting from my mob-self?

When it comes to the so-called obscene words, I should say that hardly one person in a million escapes mob-reaction. The first reaction is almost sure to be mob-reaction, mob-indignation, mob-condemnation. And the mob gets no further. But the real individual has second thoughts and says: Am I really shocked? Do I *really* feel outraged and indignant? And the answer of any individual is bound to be: No, I am not shocked, not outraged, nor indignant. I know the word, and take it for what it is, and I am not going to be jockeyed into making a mountain out of a mole-hill, not for all the law in the world.

Now if the use of a few so-called obscene words will startle man or woman out of a mob-habit into an individual state, well and good. And word prudery is so universal a mob-habit that it is time we were startled out of it.

But still we have only tackled obscenity, and the problem of pornography goes even deeper. When a man is startled into his individual self, he still may not be able to know, inside himself, whether Rabelais is or is not pornographic: and over Aretino or even Boccaccio he may perhaps puzzle in vain, torn between different emotions.

One essay on pornography, I remember, comes to the conclusion that pornography in art is that which is calculated to arouse sexual desire, or sexual excitement. And stress is laid on the fact, whether the author or artist *intended* to arouse sexual feelings. It is the old vexed question of intention, become so dull today, when we know how strong and influential our unconscious intentions are. And why a man should be held guilty of his conscious intentions, and innocent of his unconscious intentions, I don't know, since every man is more made up of unconscious intentions than of conscious ones. I am what I am, not merely what I think I am.

However! We take it, I assume, that *pornography* is something base, something unpleasant. In short, we don't like it. And why don't we like it? Because it arouses sexual feelings?

I think not. No matter how hard we may pretend otherwise, most of us rather like a moderate rousing of our sex. It warms us, stimulates us like sunshine on a grey day. After a century or two of Puritanism, this is still true of most people. Only the mob-habit of condemning any form of sex is too strong to let us admit it naturally. And there are, of course, many people who are genuinely repelled by the simplest and most natural stirrings of sexual feeling. But these people are perverts who have fallen into hatred of their fellow men: thwarted, disappointed, unfulfilled people, of whom, alas, our civilization contains so many. And they nearly always enjoy some unsimple and unnatural form of sex excitement, secretly.

Even quite advanced art critics would try to make us believe that any picture or book which had "sex appeal" was *ipso facto* a bad book or picture. This is just canting hypocrisy. Half the great poems, pictures, music, stories of the whole world are great by virtue of the beauty of their sex appeal. Titian or Renoir, the Song of Solomon or *Jane Eyre,* Mozart or "Annie Laurie," the loveliness is all interwoven with sex appeal, sex stimulus, call it what you will. Even Michelangelo, who rather hated sex, can't help filling the Cornucopia with phallic acorns. Sex is a very powerful, beneficial, and necessary stimulus in human life, and we are all grateful when we feel its warm, natural flow through us, like a form of sunshine.

So we can dismiss the idea that sex appeal in art is pornography. It may be so to the grey Puritan, but the grey Puritan is a sick man, soul and body sick, so why should we bother about his hallucinations? Sex appeal, of course, varies enormously. There are endless different kinds, and endless degrees of each kind. Perhaps it may be argued that a mild degree of sex appeal is not pornographical, whereas a high degree is. But this is a fallacy. Boccaccio at his hottest seems to me less pornographical than *Pamela* or *Clarissa Harlowe* or even *Jane Eyre,* or a host of modern books or films which pass uncensored. At the same time Wagner's *Tristan and Isolde* seems to me very near to pornography, and so, even, do some quite popular Christian hymns.

What is it, then? It isn't a question of sex appeal, merely: nor even a question of deliberate intention on the part of the author or artist to arouse sexual excitement. Rabelais sometimes had a deliberate intention, so, in a different way, did Boccaccio. And I'm sure poor Charlotte Brontë, or the authoress of *The Sheik,* did *not* have any deliberate intention to stimulate sex feelings in the reader. Yet I find *Jane Eyre* verging towards pornography and Boccaccio seems to me always fresh and wholesome.

The late British Home Secretary, who prides himself on being a very sincere Puritan, grey, grey in every fibre, said with indignant sorrow in one of his outbursts on improper books: "— and these two young people, who had been perfectly pure up till that time, after reading this book went and had sexual intercourse together! ! !" *One up to them!* is all we can answer. But the grey Guardian of British Morals seemed to think that if they had murdered one another, or worn each other to rags of nervous prostration, it would have been much better. The grey disease!

Then what is pornography, after all this? It isn't sex appeal or sex stimulus in art. It isn't even a deliberate intention on the part of the artist to arouse or to excite sexual feelings. There's nothing wrong with sexual feelings in themselves, so long as they are straightforward and not sneaking or sly. The right sort of sex stimulus is invaluable to human daily life. Without it the world grows grey. I would give everybody the gay Renaissance stories to read, they would help to shake off a lot of grey self-importance, which is our modern civilized disease.

But even I would censor genuine pornography, rigorously. It would not be very difficult. In the first place, genuine pornography is almost always underworld, it doesn't come into the open. In the second, you can recognize it by the insult it offers, invariably, to sex, and to the human spirit.

Pornography is the attempt to insult sex, to do dirt on it. This is unpardonable. Take the very lowest instance, the picture post-card sold underhand, by the underworld, in most cities. What I have seen of them have been of an ugliness to make you cry. The insult to the human body, the insult to a vital human relationship! Ugly and cheap they make the human nudity, ugly and degraded they make the sexual act, trivial and cheap and nasty.

It is the same with the books they sell in the underworld. They are either so ugly they make you ill, or so fatuous you can't imagine anybody but a cretin or a moron reading them, or writing them.

It is the same with the dirty limericks that people tell after dinner, or the dirty stories one hears commercial travellers telling each other in a smoke-room. Occasionally there is a really funny one, that redeems a great deal. But usually they are just ugly and repellent, and the so-called "humour" is just a trick of doing dirt on sex.

Now the human nudity of a great many modern people is just ugly and degraded, and the sexual act between modern people is just the same, merely ugly and degrading. But this is nothing to be proud of. It is the catastrophe of our civilization. I am sure no other civilization, not even the Roman, has showed such a vast proportion of ignominious and degraded nudity, and ugly, squalid dirty sex. Because no other civilization has driven sex into the underworld, and nudity to the w.c.

The intelligent young, thank Heaven, seem determined to alter in these two respects. They are rescuing their young nudity from the stuffy, pornographical hole-and-corner underworld of their elders, and they refuse to sneak about the sexual relation. This is a change the elderly grey ones of course deplore, but it is in fact a very great change for the better, and a real revolution.

But it is amazing how strong is the will in ordinary, vulgar people, to do dirt on sex. It was one of my fond illusions, when I was young, that the ordinary healthy-seeming sort of men, in railway carriages, or the smoke-room of an hotel or a Pullman, were healthy in their feelings and had a wholesome rough devil-may-care attitude towards sex. All wrong! All wrong! Experience teaches that common individuals of this sort have a disgusting attitude towards sex, a disgusting contempt of it, a disgusting desire to insult it. If such fellows have intercourse with a woman, they triumphantly feel that they have done her dirt, and now she is lower, cheaper, more contemptible than she was before.

It is individuals of this sort that tell dirty stories, carry indecent picture post-cards, and know the indecent books. This is the great pornographical class — the really common men-in-the-street and women-in-the-street. They have as great a hate and contempt of sex as the greyest Puritan, and when an appeal is made to them, they are always on the side of the angels. They insist that a film-heroine shall be a neuter, a sexless thing of washed-out purity. They insist that real sex feeling shall only be shown by the villain or villainess, low lust. They find a Titian or a Renoir really indecent, and they don't want their wives and daughters to see it.

Why? Because they have the grey disease of sex hatred, coupled with the yellow disease of dirt lust. The sex functions and the excrementory functions in the human body work so close together, yet they are, so to speak, utterly different in direction. Sex is a creative flow, the excrementory flow is towards dissolution, decreation, if we may use such a word. In the really healthy human being the distinction between the two is instant, our profoundest instincts are perhaps our instincts of opposition between the two flows.

But in the degraded human being the deep instincts have gone dead, and then the two flows become identical. *This* is the secret of really vulgar and of pornographical people: the sex flow and the excrement flow is the same thing to them. It happens when the psyche deteriorates, and the profound controlling instincts collapse. Then sex is dirt and dirt is sex, and sexual excitement becomes a playing with dirt, and any sign of sex in a woman becomes a show of her dirt. This is the condition of the common, vulgar human being whose name is legion, and who lifts his voice and it is the *Vox populi, vox Dei.* And this is the source of all pornography.

And for this reason we must admit that *Jane Eyre* or Wagner's *Tristan* are much nearer to pornography than is Boccaccio. Wagner and Charlotte Brontë were both in the state where the strongest instincts have collapsed, and sex has become something slightly obscene, to be wallowed in, but despised. Mr. Rochester's sex passion is not "respectable" till Mr. Rochester is burned, blinded, disfigured, and reduced to helpless dependence. Then, thoroughly humbled and humiliated, it may be merely admitted. All the previous titillations are slightly indecent, as in *Pamela* or *The Mill on the Floss* or *Anna Karenina*. As soon as there is sex excitement with a desire to spite the sexual feeling, to humiliate it and degrade it, the element of pornography enters.

For this reason, there is an element of pornography in nearly all nineteenth-century literature and very many so-called pure people have a nasty pornographical side to them, and never was the pornographical appetite stronger than it is today. It is a sign of a diseased condition of the body politic. But the way to treat the disease is to come out into the open with sex and sex stimulus. The real pornographer truly dislikes Boccaccio, because the fresh healthy naturalness of the Italian story-teller makes the modern pornographical shrimp feel the dirty worm he is. Today Boccaccio should be given to everybody, young or old, to read if they like. Only a natural fresh openness about sex will do any good, now we are being swamped by secret or semi-secret pornography. And perhaps the Renaissance story-tellers, Boccaccio, Lasca, and the rest, are the best antidote we can find now, just as more plasters of Puritanism are the most harmful remedy we can resort to.

The whole question of pornography seems to me a question of secrecy. Without secrecy there would be no pornography. But secrecy and modesty are two utterly different things. Secrecy has always an element of fear in it, amounting very often to hate. Modesty is gentle and reserved. Today, modesty is thrown to the winds, even in the presence of the grey guardians. But secrecy is hugged, being a vice in itself. And the attitude of the grey ones is: Dear young ladies, you may abandon all modesty, so long as you hug your dirty little secret.

This "dirty little secret" has become infinitely precious to the mob of people today. It is a kind of hidden sore or inflammation which, when rubbed or scratched, gives off sharp thrills that seem delicious. So the dirty little secret is rubbed and scratched more and more, till it becomes more and more secretly inflamed, and the nervous and psychic health of the individual is more and more impaired. One might easily say that half the love novels and half the love films today depend entirely for their success on the secret rubbing of the dirty little secret. You can call this sex excitement if you like, but it is sex excitement of a secretive, furtive sort, quite special. The plain and simple excitement, quite open and wholesome, which you find in some Boccaccio stories is not for a minute to be confused with the furtive excitement aroused by rubbing the dirty little secret in all secrecy in modern best-sellers. This furtive, sneaking, cunning rubbing of an inflamed spot in the imagination is the very quick of modern pornography, and it is a beastly and very dangerous thing. You can't so easily expose it, because of its very furtiveness and its sneaking cunning. So the cheap and popular modern love novel and love film flourishes and is even praised by moral guardians, because you get the sneaking thrill fumbling under all the purity of dainty underclothes, without one single gross word to let you know what is happening.

Without secrecy there would be no pornography. But if pornography is the result of sneaking secrecy, what is the result of pornography? What is the effect on the individual?

The effect on the individual is manifold, and always pernicious. But one effect is perhaps inevitable. The pornography of today, whether it be the pornography of the rubber-goods shop or the pornography of the popular novel, film, and play, is an invariable stimulant to the vice of self-abuse, onanism, masturbation, call it what you will. In young or old, man or woman, boy or girl, modern pornography is a direct provocative of masturbation. It cannot be otherwise. When the grey ones wail that the young man and the young woman went and had sexual intercourse, they are bewailing the fact that the young man and the young woman didn't go separately and masturbate. Sex must go somewhere, especially in young people. So, in our glorious civilization, it goes in masturbation. And the mass of our popular literature, the bulk of our popular amusements just exists to provoke masturbation. Masturbation is the one thoroughly secret act of the human being, more secret even than excrementation. It is the one functional result of sex secrecy, and it is stimulated and provoked by our glorious popular literature of pretty pornography, which rubs on the dirty secret without letting you know what is happening.

Now I have heard men, teachers and clergymen, commend masturbation as the solution of an otherwise insoluble sex problem. This at least is honest. The sex problem is there, and you can't just will it away. There it is, and under the ban of secrecy and taboo in mother and father, teacher, friend, and foe, it has found its own solution, the solution of masturbation.

But what about the solution? Do we accept it? Do all the grey ones of this world accept it? If so, they must now accept it openly. We can none of us pretend any longer to be blind to the fact of masturbation in young and old, man and woman. The moral guardians who are prepared to censor all open and plain portrayal of sex must now be made to give their only justification: We prefer that the people shall masturbate. If this preference is open and declared, then the existing forms of censorship are justified. If the moral guardians prefer that the people shall masturbate, then their present behaviour is correct, and popular amusements are as they should be. If sexual intercourse is deadly sin, and masturbation is comparatively pure and harmless, then all is well. Let things continue as they now are.

Is masturbation so harmless, though? Is it even comparatively pure and harmless? Not to my thinking. In the young, a certain amount of masturbation is inevitable, but not therefore natural. I thing there is no boy or girl who masturbates without feeling a sense of shame, anger, and futility. Following the excitement comes the shame, anger, humiliation, and the sense of futility. This sense of futility and humiliation deepens as the years go on, into a suppressed rage, because of the impossibility of escape. The one thing that it seems impossible to escape from, once the habit is formed, is masturbation. It goes on and on, on into old age, in spite of marriage or love affairs or anything else. And it always carries this secret feeling of futility and humiliation, futility and humiliation. And this is, perhaps, the deepest and most dangerous cancer of our civilization. Instead of being a comparatively pure and harmless vice, masturbation is certainly the most dangerous sexual vice that a society can be afflicted with, in the long run. Comparatively pure it may be — purity being what it is. But harmless! ! !

The great danger of masturbation lies in its merely exhaustive nature. In sexual intercourse, there is a give and take. A new stimulus enters as the native stimulus departs. Something quite new is added as the old surcharge is removed. And this is so in all sexual intercourse where two creatures are concerned, even in the homosexual intercourse. But in masturbation there is nothing but loss. There is no reciprocity. There is merely the spending away of a certain force, and no return. The body remains, in a sense, a corpse, after the act of self-abuse. There is no change, only deadening. There is what we call dead loss. And this is not the case in any act of sexual intercourse between two people. Two people may destroy one another in sex. But they cannot just produce the null effect of masturbation.

The only positive effect of masturbation is that it seems to release a certain mental energy, in some people. But it is mental energy which manifests itself always in the same way, in a vicious circle of analysis and impotent criticism, or else a vicious circle of false and easy sympathy, sentimentalities. The sentimentalism and the niggling analysis, often self-analysis, of most of our modern literature, is a sign of self-abuse. It is the manifestation of masturbation, the sort of conscious activity stimulated by masturbation, whether male or female. The outstanding feature of such consciousness is that there is no real object, there is only subject. This is just the same whether it be a novel or a work of science. The author never escapes from himself, he pads along within the vicious circle of himself. There is hardly a writer living who gets out of the vicious circle of himself — or a painter either. Hence the lack of creation, and the stupendous amount of production. It is a masturbation result, within the vicious circle of the self. It is self-absorption made public.

And of course the process is exhaustive. The real masturbation of Englishmen began only in the nineteenth century. It has continued with an increasing emptying of the real vitality and the real *being* of men, till now people are little more than shells of people. Most of the responses are dead, most of the awareness is dead, nearly all the constructive activity is dead, and all that remains is a sort of shell, a half-empty creature fatally self-preoccupied and incapable of either giving or taking. Incapable either of giving or taking, in the vital self. And this is masturbation result. Enclosed within the vicious circle of the self, with no vital contacts outside, the self becomes emptier and emptier, till it is almost a nullus, a nothingness.

But null or nothing as it may be, it still hangs on to the dirty little secret, which it must still secretly rub and inflame. Forever the vicious circle. And it has a weird, blind will of its own.

One of my most sympathetic critics wrote: "If Mr. Lawrence's attitude to sex were adopted, then two things would disappear, the love lyric and the smoking-room story." And this, I think, is true. But it depends on which love-lyric he means. If it is the: *Who is Sylvia, what is she?* — then it may just as well disappear. All that pure and noble and heaven-blessed stuff is only the counterpart to the smoking-room story. *Du bist wie eine Blume!* Jawohl! One can see the elderly gentleman laying his hands on

the head of the pure maiden and praying God to keep her forever so pure, so clean and beautiful. Very nice for him! Just pornography! Tickling the dirty little secret and rolling his eyes to
heaven. He knows perfectly well that if God keeps the maiden
so clean and pure and beautiful — in his vulgar sense of clean
and pure — for a few more years, then she'll be an unhappy old
maid, and not pure nor beautiful at all, only stale and pathetic.
Sentimentality is a sure sign of pornography. Why should "sadness strike through the heart" of the old gentleman, because the
maid was pure and beautiful? Anybody but a masturbator would
have been glad and would have thought: What a lovely bride for
some lucky man! — But no, not the self-enclosed, pornographic
masturbator. Sadness has to strike into his beastly heart! — Away
with such love-lyrics, we've had too much of their pornographic
poison, tickling the dirty little secret and rolling the eyes to heaven.

But if it is a question of the sound love lyric, *My love is like
a red, red rose*—! then we are on other ground. My love is like a
red, red rose only when she's *not* like a pure, pure lily. And nowadays the pure, pure lilies are mostly festering, anyhow. Away
with them and their lyrics. Away with the pure, pure lily lyric,
along with the smoking-room story. They are counterparts, and
the one is as pornographic as the other. *Du bist wie eine Blume*
is really as pornographic as a dirty story: tickling the dirty little
secret and rolling the eyes to heaven. But oh, if only Robert Burns
had been accepted for what he is, then love might still have been
like a red, red rose.

The vicious circle, the vicious circle! The vicious circle of masturbation! The vicious circle of self-consciousness that is never *fully*
self-conscious, never fully and openly conscious, but always harping
on the dirty little secret. The vicious circle of secrecy, in parents,
teachers, friends — everybody. The specially vicious circle of family.
The vast conspiracy of secrecy in the press, and at the same time,
the endless tickling of the dirty little secret. The endless masturbation! and the endless purity! The vicious circle!

How to get out of it? There is only one way: Away with the
secret! No more secrecy! The only way to stop the terrible mental
itch about sex is to come out quite simply and naturally into the
open with it. It is terribly difficult, for the secret is cunning as a
crab. Yet the thing to do is to make a beginning. The man who
said to his exasperating daughter: "My child, the only pleasure I
ever had out of you was the pleasure I had in begetting you"
has already done a great deal to release both himself and her from
the dirty little secret.

How to get out of the dirty little secret! It is, as a matter of fact, extremely difficult for us secretive moderns. You can't do it by being wise and scientific about it, like Dr. Marie Stopes: though to be wise and scientific like Dr. Marie Stopes is better than to be utterly hypocritical, like the grey ones. But by being wise and scientific in the serious and earnest manner you only tend to disinfect the dirty little secret, and either kill sex altogether with too much seriousness and intellect, or else leave it a miserable disinfected secret. The unhappy "free and pure" love of so many people who have taken out the dirty little secret and thoroughly disinfected it with scientific words is apt to be more pathetic even than the common run of dirty-little-secret love. The danger is, that in killing the dirty little secret, you kill dynamic sex altogether, and leave only the scientific and deliberate mechanism.

This is what happens to many of those who become seriously "free" in their sex, free and pure. They have mentalized sex till it is nothing at all, nothing at all but a mental quantity. And the final result is disaster, every time.

The same is true, in an even greater proportion, of the emancipated bohemians: and very many of the young are bohemian today, whether they ever set foot in Bohemia or not. But the bohemian is "sex free." The dirty little secret is no secret either to him or her. It is, indeed, a most blatantly open question. There is nothing they don't say: everything that can be revealed is revealed. And they do as they wish.

And then what? They have apparently killed the dirty little secret, but somehow they have killed everything else too. Some of the dirt still sticks, perhaps; sex remains still dirty. But the thrill of secrecy is gone. Hence the terrible dreariness and depression of modern Bohemia, and the inward dreariness and emptiness of so many young people of today. They have killed, they imagine, the dirty little secret. The thrill of secrecy is gone. Some of the dirt remains. And for the rest, depression, inertia, lack of life. For sex is the fountain-head of our energetic life, and now the fountain ceases to flow.

Why? For two reasons. The idealists along the Marie Stopes line, and the young bohemians of today have killed the dirty little secret as far as their personal self goes. But they are still under its dominion socially. In the social world, in the press, in literature, film, theatre, wireless, everywhere purity and the dirty little secret reign supreme. At home, at the dinner table, it is just the same. It is the same wherever you go. The young girl, and the young woman, is by tacit assumption pure, virgin, sexless. *Du bist wie eine*

Blume. She, poor thing, knows quite well that flowers, even lilies, have tippling yellow anthers and a sticky stigma, sex, rolling sex. But to the popular mind flowers are sexless things, and when a girl is told she is like a flower, it means she is sexless and ought to be sexless. She herself knows quite well she isn't sexless and she isn't merely like a flower. But how bear up against the great social lie forced on her? She can't! She succumbs, and the dirty little secret triumphs. She loses her interest in sex, as far as men are concerned, but the vicious circle of masturbation and self-consciousness encloses her even still faster.

This is one of the disasters of young life today. Personally, and among themselves, a great many, perhaps a majority of the young people of today, have come out into the open with sex and laid salt on the tail of the dirty little secret. And this is a very good thing. But in public, in the social world, the young are still entirely under the shadow of the grey elderly ones. The grey elderly ones belong to the last century, the eunuch century, the century of the mealy-mouthed lie, the century that has tried to destroy humanity, the nineteenth century. All our grey ones are left over from this century. And they rule us. They rule us with the grey, mealy-mouthed, canting lie of that great century of lies which, thank God, we are drifting away from. But they rule us still with the lie, for the lie, in the name of the lie. And they are too heavy and too numerous, the grey ones. It doesn't matter what government it is. They are all grey ones, left over from the last century, the century of mealy-mouthed liars, the century of purity and the dirty little secret.

So there is one cause for the depression of the young: the public reign of the mealy-mouthed lie, purity and the dirty little secret, which they themselves have privately overthrown. Having killed a good deal of the lie in their own private lives, the young are still enclosed and imprisoned within the great public lie of the grey ones. Hence the excess, the extravagance, the hysteria, and then the weakness, the feebleness, the pathetic silliness of the modern youth. They are all in a sort of prison, the prison of a great lie and a society of elderly liars. And this is one of the reasons, perhaps the main reason, why the sex flow is dying out of the young, the real energy is dying away. They are enclosed within a lie, and the sex won't flow. For the length of a complete lie is never more than three generations, and the young are the fourth generation of the nineteenth-century lie.

The second reason why the sex flow is dying is, of course, that the young, in spite of their emancipation, are still enclosed within the vicious circle of self-conscious masturbation. They are thrown back into it, when they try to escape, by the enclosure of the vast public lie of purity and the dirty little secret. The most emancipated bohemians, who swank most about sex, are still utterly self-conscious and enclosed within the Narcissus-masturbation circle. They have perhaps less sex even than the grey ones. The whole thing has been driven up into their heads. There isn't even the lurking hole of a dirty little secret. Their sex is more mental than their arithmetic; and as vital physical creatures they are more non-existent than ghosts. The modern bohemian is indeed a kind of ghost, not even Narcissus, only the image of Narcissus reflected on the face of the audience. The dirty little secret is most difficult to kill. You may put it to death publicly a thousand times, and still it reappears, like a crab, stealthily from under the submerged rocks of the personality. The French, who are supposed to be so open about sex, will perhaps be the last to kill the dirty little secret. Perhaps they don't want to. Anyhow, mere publicity won't do it.

You may parade sex abroad, but you will not kill the dirty little secret. You may read all the novels of Marcel Proust, with everything there in all detail. Yet you will not kill the dirty little secret. You will perhaps only make it more cunning. You may even bring about a state of utter indifference and sex inertia, still without killing the dirty little secret. Or you may be the most wispy and enamoured little Don Juan of modern days, and still the core of your spirit merely be the dirty little secret. That is to say, you will still be in the Narcissus-masturbation circle, the vicious circle of self-enclosure. For whenever the dirty little secret exists, it exists as the centre of the vicious circle of masturbation self-enclosure. And whenever you have the vicious circle of masturbation self-enclosure, you have at the core the dirty little secret. And the most high-flown sex-emancipated young people today are perhaps the most fatally and nervously enclosed within the masturbation self-enclosure. Nor do they want to get out of it, for there would be nothing left to come out.

But some people surely do want to come out of the awful self-enclosure. Today practically everybody is self-conscious and imprisoned in self-consciousness. It is the joyful result of the dirty little secret. Vast numbers of people don't want to come out of the prison of their self-consciousness: they have so little left to come out with. But some people, surely, want to escape this doom of self-enclosure which is the doom of our civilization. There is surely a proud minority that wants once and for all to be free of the dirty little secret.

And the way to do it is, first, to fight the sentimental lie of purity and the dirty little secret wherever you meet it, inside yourself or in the world outside. Fight the great lie of the nineteenth century, which has soaked through our sex and our bones. It means fighting with almost every breath, for the lie is ubiquitous.

Then secondly, in his adventure of self-consciousness a man must come to the limits of himself and become aware of something beyond him. A man must be self-conscious enough to know his own limits, and to be aware of that which surpasses him. What surpasses me is the very urge of life that is within me, and this life urges me to forget myself and to yield to the stirring half-born impulse to smash up the vast lie of the world, and make a new world. If my life is merely to go on in a vicious circle of self-enclosure, masturbating self-consciousness, it is worth nothing to me. If my individual life is to be enclosed within the huge corrupt lie of society today, purity and the dirty little secret, then it is worth not much to me. Freedom is a very great reality. But it means, above all things, freedom from lies. It is first, freedom from myself, from the lie of myself, from the lie of my all-importance, even to myself; it is freedom from the self-conscious masturbating thing I am, self-enclosed. And second, freedom from the vast lie of the social world, the lie of purity and the dirty little secret. All the other monstrous lies lurk under the cloak of this one primary lie. The monstrous lie of money lurks under the cloak of purity. Kill the purity lie, and the money lie will be defenceless.

We have to be sufficiently conscious, and self-conscious, to know our own limits and to be aware of the greater urge within us and beyond us. Then we cease to be primarily interested in ourselves. Then we learn to leave ourselves alone, in all the affective centres: not to force our feelings in any way, and never to force our sex. Then we make the great onslaught onto the outside lie, the inside lie being settled. And that is freedom and the fight for freedom.

The greatest of all lies in the modern world is the lie of purity and the dirty little secret. The grey ones left over from the nineteenth century are the embodiment of this lie. They dominate in society, in the press, in literature, everywhere. And, naturally, they lead the vast mob of the general public along with them.

Which means, of course, perpetual censorship of anything that would militate against the lie of purity and the dirty little secret, and perpetual encouragement of what may be called permissible pornography, pure, but tickling the dirty little secret under the delicate underclothing. The grey ones will pass and will commend floods of evasive pornography, and will suppress every outspoken word.

The law is a mere figment. In his article on the "Censorship of Books," in the *Nineteenth Century,* Viscount Brentford, the late Home Secretary, says: "Let it be remembered that the publishing of an obscene book, the issue of an obscene post-card or pornographic photograph — are all offences against the law of the land, and the Secretary of State who is the general authority for the maintenance of law and order most clearly and definitely cannot discriminate between one offence and another in discharge of his duty."

So he winds up, *ex cathedra* and infallible. But only ten lines above he has written: "I agree, that if the law were pushed to its logical conclusion, the printing and publication of such books as *The Decameron,* Benvenuto Cellini's *Life,* and Burton's *Arabian Nights* might form the subject of proceedings. But the ultimate sanction of all law is public opinion, and I do not believe for one moment that prosecution in respect of books that have been in circulation for many centuries would command public support."

Ooray then for public opinion! It only needs that a few more years shall roll. But now we see that the Secretary of State most clearly and definitely *does* discriminate between one offence and another in discharge of his duty. Simple and admitted discrimination on his part! Yet what is this public opinion? Just more lies on the part of the grey ones. They would suppress Benvenuto tomorrow, if they dared. But they would make laughing-stocks of themselves, because *tradition* backs up Benvenuto. It isn't public opinion at all. It is the grey ones afraid of making still bigger fools of themselves. But the case is simple. If the grey ones are going to be backed by a general public, then every new book that would smash the mealy-mouthed lie of the nineteenth century will be suppressed as it appears. Yet let the grey ones beware. The general public is nowadays a very unstable affair, and no longer loves its grey ones so dearly, with their old lie. And there is another public, the small public of the minority, which hates the lie and the grey ones that perpetuate the lie, and which has its own dynamic ideas about pornography and obscenity. You can't fool all the people all the time, even with purity and a dirty little secret.

And this minority public knows well that the books of many contemporary writers, both big and lesser fry, are far more pornographical than the liveliest story in *The Decameron*: because they tickle the dirty little secret and excite to private masturbation, which the wholesome Boccaccio never does. And the minority public knows full well that the most obscene painting on a Greek vase — "Thou still unravished bride of quietness" — is not as pornographical as the close-up kisses on the film, which excite men and women to secret and separate masturbation.

And perhaps one day even the general public will desire to look the thing in the face, and see for itself the difference between the sneaking masturbation pornography of the press, the film, and present-day popular literature, and then the creative portrayals of the sexual impulse that we have in Boccaccio or the Greek vase-paintings or some Pompeiian art, and which are necessary for the fulfilment of our consciousness.

As it is, the public mind is today bewildered on this point, bewildered almost to idiocy. When the police raided my picture show, they did not in the least know what to take. So they took every picture where the smallest bit of the sex organ of either man or woman showed. Quite regardless of subject or meaning or anything else: they would allow anything, these dainty policemen in a picture show, except the actual sight of a fragment of the human *pudenda*. This was the police test. The dabbing on of a postage stamp — especially a green one that could be called a leaf — would in most cases have been quite sufficient to satisfy this "public opinion."

It is, we can only repeat, a condition of idiocy. And if the purity-with-a-dirty-little-secret lie is kept up much longer, the mass of society will really be an idiot, and a dangerous idiot at that. For the public is made up of individuals. And each individual has sex, and is pivoted on sex. And if, with purity and dirty little secrets you drive every individual into the masturbation self-enclosure, and keep him there, then you will produce a state of general idiocy. For the masturbation self-enclosure produces idiots. Perhaps if we are all idiots, we shan't know it. But God preserve us.

A Propos of *Lady Chatterley's Lover*

Owing to the existence of various pirated editions of *Lady Chatterley's Lover,* I brought out in 1929 a cheap popular edition, produced in France and offered to the public at sixty francs, hoping at least to meet the European demand. The pirates, in the United States certainly, were prompt and busy. The first stolen edition was being sold in New York almost within a month of the arrival in America of the first genuine copies from Florence. It was a facsimile of the original, produced by the photographic method, and was sold, even by reliable booksellers, to the unsuspecting public as if it were the original first edition. The price was usually fifteen dollars, whereas the price of the original was ten dollars: and the purchaser was left in fond ignorance of the fraud.

This gallant attempt was followed by others. I am told there was still another facsimile edition produced in New York or Philadelphia: and I myself possess a filthy-looking book bound in a dull orange cloth, with green label, smearily produced by photography, and containing my signature forged by the little boy of the piratical family. It was when this edition appeared in London, from New York, towards the end of 1928, and was offered to the public at thirty shillings, that I put out from Florence my little second edition of two hundred copies, which I offered at a guinea. I had wanted to save it for a year or more, but had to launch it against the dirty orange pirate. But the number was too small. The orange pirate persisted.

Then I have had in my hand a very funereal volume, bound in black and elongated to look like a Bible or long hymn-book, gloomy. This time the pirate was not only sober, but earnest. He has not one but two title-pages, and on each is a vignette representing the American Eagle, with six stars round his head and lightning splashing from his paw, all surrounded by a laurel wreath in honour of his latest exploit in literary robbery. Altogether it is a sinister volume—like Captain Kidd with his face blackened, reading a sermon to those about to walk the plank. Why the pirate should have elongated the page, by adding a false page-heading, I don't know. The effect is peculiarly depressing, sinisterly high-brow. For of course this book also was produced by the photographic process. The signature anyhow is omitted. And I am told this lugubrious tome sells for ten, twenty, thirty, and fifty dollars, according to the whim of the bookseller and the gullibility of the purchaser.

That makes three pirated editions in the United States for certain. I have heard mentioned the report of a fourth, another facsimile of the original. But since I haven't seen it, I want not to believe in it.

There is, however, the European pirated edition of fifteen hundred, produced by a Paris firm of booksellers, and stamped *Imprimé en Allemagne*: Printed in Germany. Whether printed in Germany or not, it was certainly printed, not photographed, for some of the spelling errors of the original are corrected. And it is a very respectable volume, a very close replica of the original, but lacking the signature, and it gives itself away also by the green-and-yellow silk edge of the back-binding. This edition is sold to the trade at one hundred francs, and offered to the public at three hundred, four hundred, five hundred francs. Very unscrupulous booksellers are said to have forged the signature and offered the book as the original signed edition. Let us hope it is not true. But it all sounds very black against the "trade." Still there is some relief. Certain booksellers will not handle the pirated edition at all. Both sentimental and business scruples prevent them. Others handle it, but not very warmly. And apparently they would all rather handle the authorized edition. So that sentiment does genuinely enter in, against the pirates, even if not strong enough to keep them out altogether.

None of these pirated editions has received any sort of authorization from me, and from none of them have I received a penny. A semi-repentant bookseller of New York did, however, send me some dollars which were, he said, my 10% royalty on all copies sold in his shop. "I know," he wrote, "it is but a drop in the bucket." He meant of course, a drop out of the bucket. And since, for a drop, it was quite a nice little sum, what a beautiful bucketful there must have been for the pirates!

I received a belated offer from the European pirates, who found the booksellers stiff-necked, offering me a royalty on all copies sold in the past as well as the future, if I would authorize their edition. Well, I thought to myself, in a world of: Do him or you will be done by him — why not? When it came to the point, however, pride rebelled. It is understood that Judas is always ready with a kiss. But that I should have to kiss him back — !

So I managed to get published the little cheap French edition, photographed down from the original, and offered at sixty francs. English publishers urge me to make an expurgated edition, promising large returns, perhaps even a little bucket, one of those children's sea-side pails! — and insisting that I should show the public that here is a fine novel, apart from all "purple" and all "words." So I begin to be tempted and start in to expurgate. But impossible! I might as well try to clip my own nose into shape with scissors. The book bleeds.

And in spite of all antagonism, I put forth this novel as an honest, healthy book, necessary for us today. The words that shock so much at first don't shock at all after a while. Is this because the mind is depraved by habit? Not a bit. It is that the words merely shocked the eye, they never shocked the mind at all. People without minds may go on being shocked, but they don't matter. People with minds realize that they aren't shocked, and never really were: and they experience a sense of relief.

And that is the whole point. We are today, as human beings, evolved and cultured far beyond the taboos which are inherent in our culture. This is a very important fact to realize. Probably, to the Crusaders, mere words were potent and evocative to a degree we can't realize. The evocative power of the so-called obscene words must have been very dangerous to the dim-minded, obscure, violent natures of the Middle Ages, and perhaps is still too strong for slow-minded, half-evoked lower natures today. But real culture makes us give to a word only those mental and imaginative reactions which belong to the mind, and saves us from violent and indiscriminate physical reactions which may wreck social decency. In the past, man was too weak-minded, or crude-minded, to contemplate his own physical body and physical functions, without getting all messed up with physical reactions that overpowered him. It is no longer so. Culture and civilization have taught us to separate the reactions. We now know the act does not necessarily follow on the thought. In fact, thought and action, word and deed, are two separate forms of consciousness, two separate lives which we lead. We need, very sincerely, to keep a connection. But while we think, we do not act, and while we act we do not think. The great necessity is that we should act according to our thoughts, and think according to our acts. But while we are in thought we cannot really act, and while we are in action we cannot really think.

The two conditions, of thought and action, are mutually exclusive. Yet they should be related in harmony.

And this is the real point of this book. I want men and women to be able to think sex, fully, completely, honestly, and cleanly.

Even if we can't act sexually to our complete satisfaction, let us at least think sexually, complete and clear. All this talk of young girls and virginity, like a blank white sheet on which nothing is written, is pure nonsense. A young girl and a young boy is a tormented tangle, a seething confusion of sexual feelings and sexual thoughts which only the years will disentangle. Years of honest thoughts of sex, and years of struggling action in sex will bring us at last where we want to get, to our real and accomplished chastity, our completeness, when our sexual act and our sexual thought are in harmony, and the one does not interfere with the other.

Far be it from me to suggest that all women should go running after gamekeepers for lovers. Far be it from me to suggest that they should be running after anybody. A great many men and women today are happiest when they abstain and stay sexually apart, quite clean: and at the same time, when they understand and realize sex more fully. Ours is the day of realization rather than action. There has been so much action in the past, especially sexual action, a wearying repetition over and over, without a corresponding thought, a corresponding realization. Now our business is to realize sex. Today the full conscious realization of sex is even more important than the act itself. After centuries of obfuscation, the mind demands to know and know fully. The body is a good deal in abeyance, really. When people act in sex, nowadays, they are half the time acting up. They do it because they think it is expected of them. Whereas as a matter of fact it is the mind which is interested, and the body has to be provoked. The reason being that our ancestors have so assiduously acted sex without ever thinking it or realizing it, that now the act tends to be mechanical, dull and disappointing, and only fresh mental realization will freshen up the experience.

The mind has to catch up, in sex: indeed, in all the physical acts. Mentally, we lag behind in our sexual thought, in a dimness, a lurking, grovelling fear which belongs to our raw, somewhat bestial ancestors. In this one respect, sexual and physical, we have left the mind unevolved. Now we have to catch up, and make a balance between the consciousness of the body's sensations and experiences, and these sensations and experiences themselves. Balance up the consciousness of the act, and the act itself. Get the two in harmony. It means having a proper reverence for sex, and a proper awe of the body's strange experience. It means being able to use the so-called obscene words, because these are a natural part of the mind's consciousness of the body. Obscenity only comes in when the mind despises and fears the body, and the body hates and resists the mind.

When we read of the case of Colonel Barker, we see what is the matter. Colonel Barker was a woman who masqueraded as a man. The "Colonel" married a wife, and lived five years with her in "conjugal happiness." And the poor wife thought all the time she was married normally and happily to a real husband. The revelation at the end is beyond all thought cruel for the poor woman. The situation is monstrous. Yet there are thousands of women today who might be so deceived, and go on being deceived. Why? Because they know nothing, they can't think sexually at all; they are morons in this respect. It is better to give all girls this book, at the age of seventeen.

The same with the case of the venerable schoolmaster and clergyman, for years utterly "holy and good": and at the age of sixty-five, tried in the police courts for assaulting little girls. This happens at the moment when the Home Secretary, himself growing elderly, is most loudly demanding and enforcing a mealy-mouthed silence about sexual matters. Doesn't the experience of that other elderly, most righteous and "pure" gentleman, make him pause at all?

But so it is. The mind has an old grovelling fear of the body and the body's potencies. It is the mind we have to liberate, to civilize on these points. The mind's terror of the body has probably driven more men mad than ever could be counted. The insanity of a great mind like Swift's is at least partly traceable to this cause. In the poem to his mistress Celia, which has the maddened refrain, "But — Celia, Celia, Celia s***s" (the word rhymes with spits), we see what can happen to a great mind when it falls into panic. A great wit like Swift could not see how ridiculous he made himself. Of course Celia s***s! Who doesn't? And how much worse if she didn't. It is hopeless. And then think of poor Celia, made to feel iniquitous about her proper natural function, by her "lover." It is monstrous. And it comes from having taboo words, and from not keeping the mind sufficiently developed in physical and sexual consciousness.

In contrast to the Puritan hush! hush!, which produces the sexual moron, we have the modern young jazzy and high-brow person who has gone one better, and won't be hushed in any respect, and just "does as she likes." From fearing the body, and denying its existence, the advanced young go to the other extreme and treat it as a sort of toy to be played with, a slightly nasty toy, but still you can get some fun out of it, before it lets you down. These young people scoff at the importance of sex, take it like a cocktail, and flout their elders with it. These young ones are advanced and superior. They despise a book like *Lady Chatterley's Lover*. It is much too simple and ordinary for them. The naughty words they care nothing about, and the attitude to love they find old-fashioned. Why make a fuss about it? Take it like a cocktail! The book, they say, shows the mentality of a boy of fourteen. But perhaps the mentality of a boy of fourteen, who still has a little natural awe and proper fear in fact of sex, is more wholesome than the mentality of the young cocktaily person who has no respect for anything and whose mind has nothing to do but play with the toys of life, sex being one of the chief toys, and who loses his mind in the process. Heliogabalus, indeed!

So, between the stale grey Puritan who is likely to fall into sexual indecency in advanced age, and the smart jazzy person of the young world, who says: "We can do anything. If we can think a thing we can do it," and then the low uncultured person with a dirty mind, who looks for dirt — this book has hardly a space to turn in. But to them all I say the same: Keep your perversions if you like them — your perversion of Puritanism, your perversion of smart licentiousness, your perversion of a dirty mind. But I stick to my book and my position: Life is only bearable when the mind and the body are in harmony, and there is a natural balance between them, and each has a natural respect for the other.

And it is obvious, there is no balance and no harmony now. The body is at the best the tool of the mind, at the worst, the toy. The business man keeps himself "fit," that is, keeps his body in good working order, for the sake of his business, and the usual young person who spends much time on keeping fit does so as a rule out of self-conscious self-absorption, narcissism. The mind has a stereotyped set of ideas and "feelings," and the body is made to act up, like a trained dog: to beg for sugar, whether it wants sugar or whether it doesn't, to shake hands when it would dearly like to snap the hand it has to shake. The body of men and women today is just a trained dog. And of no one is this more true than of the free and emancipated young. Above all, their bodies are the bodies of trained dogs. And because the dog is trained to do things the old-fashioned dog never did, they call themselves free, full of real life, the real thing.

But they know perfectly well it is false. Just as the business man knows, somewhere, that he's all wrong. Men and women aren't really dogs: they only look like it and behave like it. Somewhere inside there is a great chagrin and a gnawing discontent. The body is, in its spontaneous natural self, dead or paralysed. It has only the secondary life of a circus dog, acting up and showing off: and then collapsing.

What life could it have, of itself? The body's life is the life of sensations and emotions. The body feels real hunger, real thirst, real joy in the sun or the snow, real pleasure in the smell of roses or the look of a lilac bush; real anger, real sorrow, real love, real tenderness, real warmth, real passion, real hate, real grief. All the emotions belong to the body, and are only recognized by the mind. We may hear the most sorrowful piece of news, and only feel a mental excitement. Then, hours after, perhaps in sleep, the awareness may reach the bodily centres, and true grief wrings the heart.

How different they are, mental feelings and real feelings. To-day, many people live and die without having had any real feelings — though they have had a "rich emotional life" apparently, having showed strong mental feeling. But it is all counterfeit. In magic, one of the so-called "occult" pictures represents a man standing, apparently, before a flat table mirror, which reflects him from the waist to the head, so that you have the man from head to waist, then his reflection downwards from waist to head again. And whatever it may mean in magic, it means what we are today, creatures whose active emotional self has no real existence, but is all reflected downwards from the mind. Our education from the start has *taught* us a certain range of emotions, what to feel and what not to feel, and how to feel the feelings we allow ourselves to feel. All the rest is just non-existent. The vulgar criticism of any new good book is: Of course nobody ever felt like that! — People allow themselves to feel a certain number of finished feelings. So it was in the last century. This feeling only what you allow yourselves to feel at last kills all capacity for feeling, and in the higher emotional range you feel nothing at all. This has come to pass in our present century. The higher emotions are strictly dead. They have to be faked.

And by the higher emotions we mean love in all its manifestations, from genuine desire to tender love, love of our fellow men, and love of God: we mean love, joy, delight, hope, true indignant anger, passionate sense of justice and injustice, truth and untruth, honour and dishonour, and real belief in *anything*: for belief is a profound emotion that has the mind's connivance. All

these things, today, are more or less dead. We have in their place
the loud and sentimental counterfeit of all such emotion.

Never was an age more sentimental, more devoid of real feeling,
more exaggerated in false feeling, than our own. Sentimentality
and counterfeit feeling have become a sort of game, everybody
trying to outdo his neighbour. The radio and the film are mere
counterfeit emotion all the time, the current press and literature
the same. People wallow in emotion: counterfeit emotion. They
lap it up: they live in it and on it. They ooze with it.

And at times, they seem to get on very well with it all. And
then, more and more, they break down. They go to pieces. You
can fool yourself for a long time about your own feelings. But not
forever. The body itself hits back at you, and hits back remorselessly
in the end.

As for other people — you can fool most people all the time, and
all people most of the time, but not all people all the time, with
false feelings. A young couple fall in counterfeit love, and fool
themselves and each other completely. But, alas, counterfeit love
is good cake but bad bread. It produces a fearful emotional indiges-
tion. Then you get a modern marriage, and a still more modern
separation.

The trouble with counterfeit emotion is that nobody is really
happy, nobody is really contented, nobody has any peace. Everybody keeps on rushing to get away from the counterfeit emotion
which is in themselves worst of all. They rush from the false feelings of Peter to the false feelings of Adrian, from the counterfeit
emotions of Margaret to those of Virginia, from film to radio,
from Eastbourne to Brighton, and the more it changes the more
it is the same thing.

Above all things love is a counterfeit feeling today. Here, above
all things, the young will tell you, is the greatest swindle. That is,
if you take it seriously. Love is all right if you take it lightly, as
an amusement. But if you begin taking it seriously you are let
down with a crash.

There are, the young women say, no *real* men to love. And
there are, the young men say, no *real* girls to fall in love with. So
they go on falling in love with unreal ones, on either side; which
means, if you can't have real feelings, you've got to have counterfeit
ones: since some feelings you've *got* to have: like falling in love.
There are still some young people who would *like* to have real
feelings, and they are bewildered to death to know why they can't.
Especially in love.

But especially in love, only counterfeit emotions exist nowadays. We have all been taught to mistrust everybody emotionally, from parents downwards, or upwards. Don't trust *anybody* with your real emotions: if you've got any: that is the slogan of today. Trust them with your money, even, but *never* with your feelings. They are bound to trample on them.

I believe there has never been an age of greater mistrust between persons than ours today: under a superficial but quite genuine social trust. Very few of my friends would pick my pocket, or let me sit on a chair where I might hurt myself. But practically all my friends would turn my real emotions to ridicule. They can't help it; it's the spirit of the day. So there goes love, and there goes friendship: for each implies a fundamental emotional sympathy. And hence, counterfeit love, which there is no escaping.

And with counterfeit emotions there is no real sex at all. Sex is the one thing you cannot really swindle; and it is the centre of the worst swindling of all, emotional swindling. Once come down to sex, and the emotional swindle must collapse. But in all the approaches to sex, the emotional swindle intensifies more and more. Till you get there. Then collapse.

Sex lashes out against counterfeit emotion, and is ruthless, devastating against false love. The peculiar hatred of people who have not loved one another, but who have pretended to, even perhaps have imagined they really did love, is one of the phenomena of our time. The phenomenon, of course, belongs to all time. But today it is almost universal. People who thought they loved one another dearly, dearly, and went on for years, ideal: lo! suddenly the most profound and vivid hatred appears. If it doesn't come out fairly young, it saves itself till the happy couple are nearing fifty, the time of the great sexual change — and then — cataclysm!

Nothing is more startling. Nothing is more staggering, in our age, than the intensity of the hatred people, men and women, feel for one another when they have once "loved" one another. It breaks out in the most extraordinary ways. And when you know people intimately, it is almost universal. It is the charwoman as much as the mistress, and the duchess as much as the policeman's wife.

And it would be too horrible, if one did not remember that in all of them, men and women alike, it is the organic reaction against counterfeit love. All love today is counterfeit. It is a stereotyped thing. All the young know just how they ought to feel and how they ought to behave, in love. And they feel and they behave like that. And it is counterfeit love. So that revenge will come back at them, ten-fold. The sex, the very sexual organism in man and woman alike accumulates a deadly and desperate rage, after a certain amount of counterfeit love has been palmed off on it, even if itself has given nothing but counterfeit love. The element of counterfeit in love at last maddens, or else kills, sex, the deepest sex in the individual. But perhaps it would be safe to say that it *always* enrages the inner sex, even if at last it kills it. There is always the period of rage. And the strange thing is, the worst offenders in the counterfeit-love game fall into the greatest rage. Those whose love has been a bit sincere are always gentler, even though they have been most swindled.

Now the real tragedy is here: that we are none of us all of a piece, none of us *all* counterfeit, or *all* true love. And in many a marriage, in among the counterfeit there flickers a little flame of the true thing, on both sides. The tragedy is, that in an age peculiarly conscious of counterfeit, peculiarly suspicious of substitute and swindle in emotion, particularly sexual emotion, the rage and mistrust against the counterfeit element is likely to overwhelm and extinguish the small, true flame of real loving communion, which might have made two lives happy. Herein lies the danger of harping only on the counterfeit and the swindle of emotion, as most "advanced" writers do. Though they do it, of course, to counterbalance the hugely greater swindle of the sentimental "sweet" writers.

Perhaps I shall have given some notion of my feeling about sex, for which I have been so monotonously abused. When a "serious" young man said to me the other day: "I can't believe in the regeneration of England by sex, you know," I could only say, "I'm sure you can't." He had no sex, anyhow: poor, self-conscious, uneasy, narcissus-monk as he was. And he didn't know what it meant, to have any. To him, people only had minds, or no minds, mostly no minds, so they were only there to be gibed at, and he wandered round ineffectively seeking for gibes or for truth, tight shut in inside his own ego.

Now when brilliant young people like this talk to me about sex: or scorn to: I say nothing. There is nothing to say. But I feel a terrible weariness. To them sex means, just plainly and simply, a lady's underclothing, and the fumbling therewith. They have read all the love literature, *Anna Karenina,* all the rest, and looked at statues and pictures of Aphrodite, all very laudable. Yet when it comes to actuality, to today, sex means to them meaningless young women and expensive underthings. Whether they are young men from Oxford, or working-men, it is the same. The story from the modish summer resort, where city ladies take up with young mountaineer "dancing partners" for a season — or less — is typical. It was end of September, the summer visitors had almost all gone. Young John, the young mountain farmer, had said good-bye to his "lady" from the capital, and was lounging about alone. "Ho, John! you'll be missing your lady!" "Nay!" he said. "Only she had such nice underclothes."

That is all sex means to them: just the trimmings. The regeneration of England with that? Good God! Poor England, she will have to regenerate the sex in her young people, before they do any regenerating of her. It isn't England that needs regeneration, it is her young.

They accuse me of barbarism. I want to drag England down to the level of savages. But it is this crude stupidity, deadness, about sex which I find barbaric and savage. The man who finds a woman's underclothing the most exciting part about her is a savage. Savages are like that. We read of the woman-savage who wore three overcoats on top of one another to excite her man: and did it. That ghastly crudity of seeing in sex nothing but a functional act and a certain fumbling with clothes is, in my opinion, a low degree of barbarism, savagery. And as far as sex goes, our white civilization is crude, barbaric, and uglily savage: especially England and America.

Witness Bernard Shaw, one of the greatest exponents of our civilization. He says clothes arouse sex and lack of clothes tends to kill sex — speaking of muffled-up women or our present barearmed and bare-legged sisters: and scoffs at the Pope for wanting to cover women up; saying that the last person in the world to know anything about sex is the Chief Priest of Europe: and that the one person to ask about it would be the Chief Prostitute of Europe, if there were such a person.

Here we see the flippancy and vulgarity of our chief thinkers, at least. The half-naked women of today certainly do not rouse much sexual feeling in the muffled-up men of today — who don't rouse much sexual feeling in the women, either. But why? Why does the bare woman of today rouse so much less sexual feeling than the muffled-up woman of Mr. Shaw's muffled-up eighties? It would be silly to make it a question of mere muffling.

When a woman's sex is in itself dynamic and alive, then it is a power in itself, beyond her reason. And of itself it emits its peculiar spell, drawing men in the first delight of desire. And the woman has to protect herself, hide herself as much as possible. She veils herself in timidity and modesty, because her sex is a power in itself, exposing her to the desire of men. If a woman in whom sex was alive and positive were to expose her naked flesh as women do today, then men would go mad for her. As David was mad for Bathsheba.

But when a woman's sex has lost its dynamic call, and is in a sense dead or static, then the woman *wants* to attract men, for the simple reason that she finds she no longer does attract them. So all the activity that used to be unconscious and delightful becomes conscious and repellent. The woman exposes her flesh more and more, and the more she exposes, the more men are sexually repelled by her. But let us not forget that the men are *socially* thrilled, while sexually repelled. The two things are opposites, today. Socially, men like the gesture of the half-naked woman, half-naked in the street. It is *chic,* it is a declaration of defiance and independence, it is modern, it is free, it is popular because it is strictly a-sexual, or anti-sexual. Neither men nor women *want* to feel real desire, today. They want the counterfeit, mental substitute.

But we are very mixed, all of us, and creatures of many diverse and often opposing desires. The very men who encourage women to be most daring and sexless complain most bitterly of the sexlessness of women. The same with women. The women who adore men so tremendously for their social smartness and sexlessness as males, hate them most bitterly for not being "men." In public, *en masse,* and socially, everybody today wants counterfeit sex. But at certain hours in their lives, all individuals hate counterfeit sex with deadly and maddened hate, and those who have dealt it out most perhaps have the wildest hate of it, in the other person — or persons.

The girls of today could muffle themselves up to the eyes, wear crinolines and chignons and all the rest, and though they would not, perhaps, have the peculiar hardening effect on the hearts of men that our half-naked women truly have, neither would they exert any more real sexual attraction. If there is no sex to muffle up, it's no good muffling. Or not much good. Man is often willing to be deceived — for a time — even by muffled-up nothingness.

The point is, when women are sexually alive and quivering and helplessly attractive, beyond their will, then they always cover themselves, and drape themselves with clothes, gracefully. The extravagance of 1880 bustles and such things was only a forewarning of approaching sexlessness.

While sex is a power in itself, women try all kinds of fascinating disguise, and men flaunt. When the Pope insists that women shall cover their naked flesh in church, it is not sex he is opposing, but the sexless tricks of female immodesty. The Pope, and the priests, conclude that the flaunting of naked women's flesh in street and church produces a bad, "unholy" state of mind both in men and women. And they are right. But not because the exposure arouses sexual desire: it doesn't, or very rarely: even Mr. Shaw knows that. But when women's flesh arouses no sort of desire, something is specially wrong! Something is sadly wrong. For the naked arms of women today arouse a feeling of flippancy, cynicism, and vulgarity which is indeed the very last feeling to go to church with, if you have any respect for the Church. The bare arms of women in an Italian church are really a mark of disrespect, given the tradition.

The Catholic Church, especially in the south, is neither anti-sexual, like the northern Churches, nor a-sexual, like Mr. Shaw and such social thinkers. The Catholic Church recognizes sex, and makes of marriage a sacrament based on the sexual communion, for the purpose of procreation. But procreation in the south is not the bare and scientific fact, and act, that it is in the north. The act of procreation is still charged with all the sensual mystery and importance of the old past. The man is potential creator, and in this has his splendour. All of which has been stripped away by the northern Churches and the Shavian logical triviality.

But all this which has gone in the north, the Church has tried to keep in the south, knowing that it is of basic importance in life. The sense of being a potential creator and law-giver, as father and husband, is perhaps essential to the day-by-day life of a man, if he is to live full and satisfied. The sense of the eternality of marriage is perhaps necessary to the inward peace, both of men and women. Even if it carry a sense of doom, it is necessary. The Catholic Church does not spend its time reminding the people that in heaven there is no marrying nor giving in marriage. It insists: if you marry, you marry forever! And the people accept the decree, the doom, and the dignity of it. To the priest, sex is the clue to marriage and marriage is the clue to the daily life of the people and the Church is the clue to the greater life.

So that sexual lure in itself is not deadly to the Church. Much more deadly is the anti-sexual defiance of bare arms and flippancy, "freedom," cynicism, irreverence. Sex may be obscene in church, or blasphemous, but never cynical and atheist. Potentially, the bare arms of women today are cynical, atheist, in the dangerous, vulgar form of atheism. Naturally the Church is against it. The Chief Priest of Europe knows more about sex than Mr. Shaw does, anyhow, because he knows more about the essential nature of the human being. Traditionally, he has a thousand years' experience.

Mr. Shaw jumped up in a day. And Mr. Shaw, as a dramatist, has jumped up to play tricks with the counterfeit sex of the modern public. No doubt he can do it. So can the cheapest film. But it is equally obvious that he *cannot* touch the deeper sex of the real individual, whose existence he hardly seems to suspect.

And, as a parallel to himself, Mr. Shaw suggests that the Chief Prostitute of Europe would be the one to consult about sex, not the Chief Priest. The parallel is just. The Chief Prostitute of Europe would know truly as much about sex as Mr. Shaw himself does. Which is, not much. Just like Mr. Shaw, the Chief Prostitute of Europe would know an immense amount about the counterfeit sex of men, the shoddy thing that is worked by tricks. And just like him, she would know nothing at all about the real sex in a man, that has the rhythm of the seasons and the years, the crisis of the winter solstice and the passion of Easter. This the Chief Prostitute would know nothing about, positively, because to be a prostitute she would have to have lost it. But even then, she would know more than Mr. Shaw. She would know that the profound, rhythmic sex of man's inward life *existed*. She would know, because time and again she would have been up against it. All the literature of the world shows the prostitute's ultimate impotence in sex, her inability to keep a man, her rage against the profound instinct of fidelity in a man, which is, as shown by world history, just a little deeper and more powerful than his instinct of faithless sexual promiscuity. All the literature of the world shows how profound is the instinct of fidelity in both man and woman, how men and women both hanker restlessly after the satisfaction of this instinct, and fret at their own inability to find the real mode of fidelity. The instinct of fidelity is perhaps the deepest instinct in the great complex we call sex. Where there is real sex there is the underlying passion for fidelity. And the prostitute knows this, because she is up against it. She can only keep men who have no real sex, the counterfeits: and these she despises. The men with real sex leave her inevitably, as unable to satisfy their real desire.

The Chief Prostitute knows so much. So does the Pope, if he troubles to think of it, for it is all in the traditional consciousness of the Church. But the Chief Dramatist knows nothing of it. He has a curious blank in his make-up. To him, all sex is infidelity and only infidelity is sex. Marriage is sexless, null. Sex is only manifested in infidelity, and the queen of sex is the Chief Prostitute. If sex crops up in marriage, it is because one party falls in love with somebody else, and wants to be unfaithful. Infidelity is sex, and prostitutes know all about it. Wives know nothing and are nothing, in that respect.

This is the teaching of the Chief Dramatists and Chief Thinkers of our generation. And the vulgar public agrees with them entirely. Sex is a thing you don't have except to be naughty with. Apart from naughtiness, that is, apart from infidelity and fornication, sex doesn't exist. Our chief thinkers, ending in the flippantly cocksure Mr. Shaw, have taught this trash so thoroughly that it has almost become a fact. Sex is almost non-existent, apart from the counterfeit forms of prostitution and shallow fornication. And marriage is empty, hollow.

Now this question of sex and marriage is of paramount importance. Our social life is established on marriage, and marriage, the sociologists say, is established upon property. Marriage has been found the best method of conserving property and stimulating production. Which is all there is to it.

But is it? We are just in the throes of a great revolt against marriage, a passionate revolt against its ties and restrictions. In fact, at least three-quarters of the unhappiness of modern life could be laid at the door of marriage. There are few married people today, and few unmarried, who have not felt an intense and vivid hatred against marriage itself, marriage as an institution and an imposition upon human life. Far greater than the revolt against governments is this revolt against marriage.

And everybody, pretty well, takes it for granted that as soon as we can find a possible way out of it, marriage will be abolished. The Soviet abolishes marriage: or did. If new "modern" states spring up, they will almost certainly follow suit. They will try to find some social substitute for marriage, and abolish the hated yoke of conjugality. State support of motherhood, State support of children, and independence of women. It is on the programme of every great scheme of reform. And it means, of course, the abolition of marriage.

The only question to ask ourselves is, do we really want it? Do we want the absolute independence of women, State support of motherhood and of children, and consequent doing away with the necessity of marriage? Do we want it? Because all that matters is that men and women shall do what they *really* want to do. Though here, as everywhere, we must remember that man has a double set of desires, the shallow and the profound, the personal, superficial, temporary desires, and the inner, impersonal, great desires that are fulfilled in long periods of time. The desires of the moment are easy to recognize, but the others, the deeper ones, are difficult. It is the business of our Chief Thinkers to tell us of our deeper desires, not to keep shrilling our little desires in our ears.

Now the Church is established upon a recognition of some, at least, of the greatest and deepest desires in man, desires that take years, or a life-time, or even centuries to fulfil. And the Church, celibate as its priesthood may be, built as it may be upon the lonely rock of Peter, or of Paul, really rests upon the indissolubility of marriage. Make marriage in any serious degree unstable, dissoluble, destroy the permanency of marriage, and the Church falls. Witness the enormous decline of the Church of England.

The reason being that the Church is established upon the element of *union* in mankind. And the first element of union in the Christian world is the marriage tie. The marriage tie, the marriage bond, take it which way you like, is the fundamental connecting link in Christian society. Break it, and you will have to go back to the overwhelming dominance of the State, which existed before the Christian era. The Roman State was all-powerful, the Roman Fathers represented the State, the Roman family was the father's estate, held more or less in fee for the State itself. It was the same in Greece, with not so much feeling for the *permanence* of property, but rather a dazzling splash of the moment's possessions. The family was much more insecure in Greece than in Rome.

But, in either case, the family was the man, as representing the State. There are States where the family is the woman: or there have been. There are States where the family hardly exists, priest States where the priestly control is everything, even functioning as family control. Then there is the Soviet State, where again family is not supposed to exist, and the State controls every individual direct, mechanically, as the great religious States, such as early Egypt, may have controlled every individual direct, through priestly surveillance and ritual.

Now the question is, do we want to go back, or forward, to any of these forms of State control? Do we want to be like the Romans under the Empire, or even under the Republic? Do we want to be, as far as our family and our freedom is concerned, like the Greek citizens of a City State in Hellas? Do we want to imagine ourselves in the strange priest-controlled, ritual-fulfilled condition of the earlier Egyptians? Do we want to be bullied by a Soviet?

For my part, I have to say NO! every time. And having said

it, we have to come back and consider the famous saying, that perhaps the greatest contribution to the social life of man made by Christianity is — marriage. Christianity brought marriage into the world: marriage as we know it. Christianity established the little autonomy of the family within the greater rule of the State. Christianity made marriage in some respects inviolate, not to be violated by the State. It is marriage, perhaps, which has given man the best of his freedom, given him his little kingdom of his own within the big kingdom of the State, given him his foothold of independence on which to stand and resist an unjust State. Man and wife, a king and queen with one or two subjects, and a few square yards of territory of their own: this, really, is marriage. It is a true freedom because it is a true fulfilment, for man, woman, and children.

Do we, then, want to break marriage? If we do break it, it means we all fall to a far greater extent under the direct sway of the State. Do we want to fall under the direct sway of the State, any State? For my part, I don't.

And the Church created marriage by making it a sacrament, a sacrament of man and woman united in the sex communion, and never to be separated, except by death. And even when separated by death, still not freed from the marriage. Marriage, as far as the individual went, eternal. Marriage, making one complete body out of two incomplete ones, and providing for the complex development of the man's soul and the woman's soul in unison, throughout a life-time. Marriage sacred and inviolable, the great way of earthly fulfilment for man and woman, in unison, under the spiritual rule of the Church.

This is Christianity's great contribution to the life of man, and it is only too easily overlooked. Is it, or is it not, a great step in the direction of life-fulfilment, for men and women? Is it, or is it not? Is marriage a great help to the fulfilment of man and woman, or is it a frustration? It is a very important question indeed, and every man and woman must answer it.

If we are to take the Nonconformist, Protestant idea of ourselves: that we are all isolated individual souls, and our supreme business is to save our own souls, then marriage surely is a hindrance. If I am only out to save my own soul, I'd better leave marriage alone. As the monks and hermits knew. But also, if I am only out to save other people's souls, I had also best leave marriage alone, as the apostles knew, and the preaching saints.

But supposing I am neither bent on saving my own soul nor other people's souls? Supposing Salvation seems incomprehensible to me, as I confess it does? "Being saved" seems to me just jargon, the jargon of self-conceit. Supposing, then, that I cannot see this Saviour and Salvation stuff, supposing that I see the soul as something which must be developed and fulfilled throughout a life-time, sustained and nourished, developed and further fulfilled, to the very end; what then?

Then I realize that marriage, or something like it, is essential, and that the old Church knew best the enduring needs of man, beyond the spasmodic needs of today and yesterday. The Church established marriage for life, for the fulfilment of the soul's living life, not postponing it till the after-death.

The old Church knew that life is here our portion, to be lived, to be lived in fulfilment. The stern rule of Benedict, the wild flights of Francis of Assisi, these were coruscations in the steady heaven of the Church. The rhythm of life itself was preserved by the Church hour by hour, day by day, season by season, year by year, epoch by epoch, down among the people, and the wild coruscations were accommodated to this permanent rhythm. We feel it, in the south, in the country, when we hear the jangle of the bells at dawn, at noon, at sunset, marking the hours with the sound of mass or prayers. It is the rhythm of the daily sun. We feel it in the festivals, the processions, Christmas, the Three Kings, Easter, Pentecost, St. John's Day, All Saints, All Souls. This is the wheeling of the year, the movement of the sun through solstice and equinox, the coming of the seasons, the going of the seasons. And it is the inward rhythm of man and woman, too, the sadness of Lent, the delight of Easter, the wonder of Pentecost, the fires of St. John, the candles on the graves of All Souls, the lit-up tree of Christmas, all representing kindled rhythmic emotions in the souls of men and women. And men experience the great rhythm of emotion man-wise, women experience it woman-wise, and in the unison of men and women it is complete.

Augustine said that God created the universe new every day: and to the living, emotional soul this is true. Every dawn dawns upon an entirely new universe, every Easter lights up an entirely new glory of a new world opening in utterly new flower. And the soul of man and the soul of woman is new in the same way, with the infinite delight of life and the ever-newness of life. So a man and a woman are new to one another throughout a life-time, in the rhythm of marriage that matches the rhythm of the year.

Sex is the balance of male and female in the universe, the attraction, the repulsion, the transit of neutrality, the new attraction, the new repulsion, always different, always new. The long neuter spell of Lent, when the blood is low, and the delight of the Easter kiss, the sexual revel of spring, the passion of midsummer, the slow recoil, revolt, and grief of autumn, greyness again, then the sharp stimulus of winter of the long nights. Sex goes through the rhythm of the year, in man and woman, ceaselessly changing: the rhythm of the sun in his relation to the earth. Oh, what a catastrophe for man when he cut himself off from the rhythm of the year, from his unison with the sun and the earth. Oh, what a catastrophe, what a maiming of love when it was made a personal, merely personal feeling, taken away from the rising and the setting of the sun, and cut off from the magic connection of the solstice and the equinox! This is what is the matter with us. We are bleeding at the roots, because we are cut off from the earth and sun and stars, and love is a grinning mockery, because, poor blossom, we plucked it from its stem on the tree of Life, and expected it to keep on blooming in our civilized vase on the table.

Marriage is the clue to human life, but there is no marriage apart from the wheeling sun and the nodding earth, from the straying of the planets and the magnificence of the fixed stars. Is not a man different, utterly different, at dawn from what he is at sunset? and a woman too? And does not the changing harmony and discord of their variation make the secret music of life?

And is it not so throughout life? A man is different at thirty, at forty, at fifty, at sixty, at seventy: and the woman at his side is different. But is there not some strange conjunction in their differences? Is there not some peculiar harmony, through youth, the period of child-birth, the period of florescence and young children, the period of the woman's change of life, painful yet also a renewal, the period of waning passion but mellowing delight of affection, the dim, unequal period of the approach of death, when the man and woman look at one another with the dim apprehension of separation that is not really a separation: is there not, throughout it all, some unseen, unknown interplay of balance, harmony, completion, like some soundless symphony which moves with a rhythm from phase to phase, so different, so very different in the various movements, and yet one symphony, made out of the soundless singing of two strange and incompatible lives, a man's and a woman's?

This is marriage, the mystery of marriage, marriage which fulfils itself here, in this life. We may well believe that in heaven there is no marrying or giving in marriage. All this has to be fulfilled here, and if it is not fulfilled here, it will never be fulfilled.

The great saints only live, even Jesus only lives to add a new fulfilment and a new beauty to the permanent sacrament of marriage.

But — and this *but* crashes through our heart like a bullet — marriage is no marriage that is not basically and permanently phallic, and that is not linked up with the sun and the earth, the moon and the fixed stars and the planets, in the rhythm of days, in the rhythm of months, in the rhythm of quarters, of years, of decades and of centuries. Marriage is no marriage that is not a correspondence of blood. For the blood is the substance of the soul, and of the deepest consciousness. It is by blood that we are: and it is by the heart and the liver that we live and move and have our being. In the blood, knowing and being, or feeling, are one and undivided: no serpent and no apple has caused a split. So that only when the conjunction is of the blood, is marriage truly marriage. The blood of man and the blood of woman are two eternally different streams, that can never be mingled. Even scientifically we know it. But therefore they are the two rivers that encircle the whole of life, and in marriage the circle is complete, and in sex the two rivers touch and renew one another, without ever commingling or confusing. We know it. The phallus is a column of blood that fills the valley of blood of a woman. The great river of male blood touches to its depths the great river of female blood — yet neither breaks its bounds. It is the deepest of all communions, as all the religions, in practice, know. And it is one of the greatest mysteries, in fact, the greatest, as almost every initiation shows, showing the supreme achievement of the mystic marriage.

And this is the meaning of the sexual act: this Communion, this touching on one another of the two rivers, Euphrates and Tigris — to use old jargon — and the enclosing of the land of Mesopotamia, where Paradise was, or the Park of Eden, where man had his beginning. This is marriage, this circuit of the two rivers, this communion of the two blood-streams, this, and nothing else: as all the religions know.

Two rivers of blood, are man and wife, two distinct eternal streams, that have the power of touching and communing and so renewing, making new one another, without any breaking of the subtle confines, any confusing or commingling. And the phallus is the connecting link between the two rivers, that establishes the two streams in a oneness, and gives out of their duality a single circuit, forever. And this, this oneness gradually accomplished throughout a life-time in twoness, is the highest achievement of

time or eternity. From it all things human spring, children and
beauty and well-made things; all the true creations of humanity.
And all we know of the will of God is that He wishes this, this
oneness, to take place, fulfilled over a lifetime, this oneness within
the great dual blood-stream of humanity.

Man dies, and woman dies, and perhaps separate the souls go
back to the Creator. Who knows? But we know that the oneness
of the blood-stream of man and woman in marriage completes
the universe, as far as humanity is concerned, completes the stream-
ing of the sun and the flowing of the stars.

There is, of course, the counterpart to all this, the counterfeit.
There is counterfeit marriage, like nearly all marriage today.
Modern people are just personalities, and modern marriage takes
place when two people are "thrilled" by each other's personality:
when they have the same tastes in furniture or books or sport or
amusement, when they love "talking" to one another, when they
admire one another's "minds." Now this, this affinity of mind and
personality is an excellent basis of friendship between the sexes,
but a disastrous basis for marriage. Because marriage inevitably
starts the sex activity, and the sex activity is, and always was and
will be, in some way hostile to the mental, *personal* relationship
between man and woman. It is almost an axiom that the marriage of two *personalities* will end in a startling physical hatred.
People who are personally devoted to one another at first end by
hating one another with a hate which they cannot account for,
which they try to hide, for it makes them ashamed, and which is
none the less only too painfully obvious, especially to one another.
In people of strong individual feeling the irritation that accumulates
in marriage increases only too often to a point of rage that is close
akin to madness. And, apparently, all without reason.

But the real reason is, that the exclusive sympathy of nerves
and mind and personal interest is, alas, hostile to blood-sympathy,
in the sexes. The modern cult of personality is excellent for friendship between the sexes, and fatal for marriage. On the whole, it
would be better if modern people didn't marry. They could remain so much more true to what they are, to their own personality.

But marriage or no marriage, the fatal thing happens. If you
have only known personal sympathy and personal love, then rage
and hatred will sooner or later take possession of the soul, because of the frustration and denial of blood-sympathy, blood-
contact. In celibacy, the denial is withering and souring, but in
marriage, the denial produces a sort of rage. And we can no more
avoid this, nowadays, than we can avoid thunder-storms. It is part

of the phenomenon of the psyche. The important point is that sex itself comes to subserve the personality and the personal "love" entirely, without ever giving sexual satisfaction or fulfilment. In fact, there is probably far more sexual activity in a "personal" marriage than in a blood-marriage. Woman sighs for a perpetual lover: and in the personal marriage, relatively, she gets him. And how she comes to hate him, with his never-ending desire, which never gets anywhere or fulfils anything!

It is a mistake I have made, talking of sex. I have always inferred that sex meant blood-sympathy and blood-contact. Technically this is so. But as a matter of fact, nearly all modern sex is a pure matter of nerves, cold and bloodless. This is personal sex. And this white, cold, nervous, "poetic" personal sex, which is practically all the sex that moderns know, has a very peculiar physiological effect, as well as psychological. The two blood-streams are brought into contact, in man and woman, just the same as in the urge of blood-passion and blood-desire. But whereas the contact in the urge of blood-desire is positive, making a newness in the blood, in the insistence of this nervous, personal desire the blood-contact becomes frictional and destructive, there is a resultant whitening and impoverishment of the blood. Personal or nervous or spiritual sex is destructive to the blood, has a katabolistic activity, whereas coition in warm blood-desire is an activity of metabolism. The katabolism of "nervous" sex activity may produce for a time a sort of ecstasy and a heightening of consciousness. But this, like the effect of alcohol or drugs, is the result of the decomposition of certain corpuscles in the blood, and is a process of impoverishment. This is one of the many reasons for the failure of energy in modern people; sexual activity, which ought to be refreshing and renewing, becomes exhaustive and debilitating. So that when the young man fails to believe in the regeneration of England by sex, I am constrained to agree with him. Since modern sex is practically all personal and nervous, and, in effect, exhaustive, disintegrative. The disintegrative effect of modern sex activity is undeniable. It is only less fatal than the disintegrative effect of masturbation, which is more deadly still.

So that at last I begin to see the point of my critics' abuse of my exalting of sex. They only know one form of sex: in fact, to them there *is* only one form of sex: the nervous, personal, disintegrative sort, the "white" sex. And this, of course, is something to be flowery and false about, but nothing to be very hopeful about. I quite agree. And I quite agree, we can have no hope of the regeneration of England from such sort of sex.

At the same time, I cannot see any hope of regeneration for a sexless England. An England that has lost its sex seems to me nothing to feel very hopeful about. And nobody feels very hopeful about it. Though I may have been a fool for insisting on sex where the current sort of sex is just what I *don't* mean and *don't* want, still I can't go back on it all and believe in the regeneration of England by pure sexlessness. A sexless England! — it doesn't ring very hopeful, to me.

And the other, the warm blood-sex that establishes the living and re-vitalizing connection between man and woman, how are we to get that back? I don't know. Yet get it back we must: or the younger ones must, or we are all lost. For the bridge to the future is the phallus, and there's the end of it. But not the poor, nervous counterfeit phallus of modern "nervous" love. Not that.

For the new impulse to life will never come without blood-contact; the true, positive blood-contact, not the nervous negative reaction. And the essential blood-contact is between man and woman, always has been so, always will be. The contact of positive sex. The homosexual contacts are secondary, even if not merely substitutes of exasperated reaction from the utterly unsatisfactory nervous sex between men and women.

If England is to be regenerated — to use the phrase of the young man who seemed to think there was need of *regeneration* — the very word is his — then it will be by the arising of a new blood-contact, a new touch, and a new marriage. It will be a phallic rather than a sexual regeneration. For the phallus is only the great old symbol of godly vitality in a man, and of immediate contact.

It will also be a renewal of marriage: the true phallic marriage. And, still further, it will be marriage set again in relationship to the rhythmic cosmos. The rhythm of the cosmos is something we cannot get away from, without bitterly impoverishing our lives. The Early Christians tried to kill the old pagan rhythm of cosmic ritual, and to some extent succeeded. They killed the planets and the zodiac, perhaps because astrology had already become debased to fortune-telling. They wanted to kill the festivals of the year. But the Church, which knows that man doth not live by man alone, but by the sun and moon and earth in their revolutions, restored the sacred days and feasts almost as the pagans had them, and the Christian peasants went on very much as the pagan peasants had gone, with the sunrise pause for worship, and the sunset, and noon, the three great daily moments of the sun: then the new holy-day, one in the ancient seven-cycle: then Easter and the dying and rising of God, Pentecost, Midsummer Fire, the November dead and the spirits of the grave, then Christmas, then Three Kings. For centuries the mass of people lived in this rhythm, under the Church. And it is down in the mass that the roots of religion are eternal. When the mass of a people loses the religious rhythm, that people is dead, without hope. But Protestantism came and gave a great blow to the religious and ritualistic rhythm of the year, in human life. Nonconformity *almost* finished the deed. Now you have a poor, blind, disconnected people with nothing but politics and bank-holidays to satisfy the eternal human need of living in ritual adjustment to the cosmos in its revolutions, in eternal submission to the greater laws. And marriage, being one of the greater necessities, has suffered the same from the loss of the sway of the greater laws, the cosmic rhythms which should sway life always. Mankind has got to get back to the rhythm of the cosmos, and the permanence of marriage.

All this is post-script, or afterthought, to my novel, *Lady Chatterley's Lover*. Man has little needs and deeper needs. We have fallen into the mistake of living from our little needs till we have almost lost our deeper needs in a sort of madness. There is a little morality, which concerns persons and the little needs of man: and this, alas, is the morality we live by. But there is a deeper morality, which concerns all womanhood, all manhood, and nations, and races, and classes of men. This greater morality affects the destiny of mankind over long stretches of time, applies to man's greater needs, and is often in conflict with the little morality of the little needs. The tragic consciousness has taught us, even, that one of the greater needs of man is a knowledge and experience of death; every man needs to know death in his own body. But the greater consciousness of the pre-tragic and post-tragic epochs teaches us — though we have not yet reached the post-tragic epoch — that the greatest need of man is the renewal forever of the complete rhythm of life and death, the rhythm of the sun's year, the body's year of a lifetime, and the greater year of the stars, the soul's year of immortality. This is our need, our imperative need. It is a need of the mind and soul, body, spirit and sex: all. It is no use asking for a Word to fulfil such a need. No Word, no Logos, no Utterance will ever do it. The Word is uttered, most of it: we need only pay true attention. But who will call us to the Deed, the great Deed of the Seasons and the year, the Deed of the soul's cycle, the Deed of a woman's life at one with a man's, the little Deed of the moon's wandering, the bigger Deed of the sun's, and the biggest, of the great still stars? It is the *Deed* of life we have now to learn: we are supposed to have learnt the Word, but, alas, look at us. Word-perfect we may be, but Deed-demented. Let us prepare now for the death of our present "little" life, and the re-emergence in a bigger life, in touch with the moving cosmos.

It is a question, practically, of relationship. We *must* get back into relation, vivid and nourishing relation to the cosmos and the universe. The way is through daily ritual, and the re-awakening. We *must* once more practise the ritual of dawn and noon and sunset, the ritual of the kindling fire and pouring water, the ritual of the first breath, and the last. This is an affair of the individual and the household, a ritual of day. The ritual of the moon in her phases, of the morning star and the evening star is for men and women separate. Then the ritual of the seasons, with the Drama and the Passion of the soul embodied in procession and dance, this is for the community, an act of men and women, a whole community, in togetherness. And the ritual of the great events in the year of stars is for nations and whole peoples. To these rituals we must return: or we must evolve them to suit our needs. For the truth is, we are perishing for lack of fulfilment of our greater needs, we are cut off from the great sources of our inward nourishment and renewal, sources which flow eternally in the universe. Vitally, the human race is dying. It is like a great uprooted tree, with its roots in the air. We must plant ourselves again in the universe.

It means a return to ancient forms. But we shall have to create these forms again, and it is more difficult than the preaching of an evangel. The Gospel came to tell us we were all saved. We look at the world today and realize that humanity, alas, instead of being saved from sin, whatever that may be, is almost completely lost, lost to life, and near to nullity and extermination. We have to go back, a long way, before the idealist conceptions begin, before Plato, before the tragic idea of life arose, to get on to our feet again. For the gospel of salvation through the Ideals and escape from the body coincided with the tragic conception of human life. Salvation and tragedy are the same thing, and they are now both beside the point.

Back, before the idealist religions and philosophies arose and started man on the great excursion of tragedy. The last three thousand years of mankind have been an excursion into ideals, bodilessness, and tragedy, and now the excursion is over. And it is like the end of a tragedy in the theatre. The stage is strewn with dead bodies, worse still, with meaningless bodies, and the curtain comes down.

But in life, the curtain never comes down on the scene. There the dead bodies lie, and the inert ones, and somebody has to clear them away, somebody has to carry on. It is the day after. Today is already the day after the end of the tragic and idealist epoch. Utmost inertia falls on the remaining protagonists. Yet we have to carry on.

Now we have to re-establish the great relationships which the grand idealists, with their underlying pessimism, their belief that life is nothing but futile conflict, to be avoided even unto death, destroyed for us. Buddha, Plato, Jesus, they were all three utter pessimists as regards life, teaching that the only happiness lay in abstracting oneself from life, the daily, yearly, seasonal life of birth and death and fruition, and in living in the "immutable" or eternal spirit. But now, after almost three thousand years, now that we are almost abstracted entirely from the rhythmic life of the seasons, birth and death and fruition, now we realize that such abstraction is neither bliss nor liberation, but nullity. It brings null inertia. And the great saviours and teachers only cut us off from life. It was the tragic *excursus*.

The universe is dead for us, and how is it to come to life again? "Knowledge" has killed the sun, making it a ball of gas, with spots; "knowledge" has killed the moon, it is a dead little earth fretted with extinct craters as with small pox; the machine has killed the earth for us, making it a surface, more or less bumpy, that you travel over. How, out of all this, are we to get back the grand orbs of the soul's heavens, that fill us with unspeakable joy? How are we to get back Apollo, and Attis, Demeter, Persephone, and the halls of Dis? How even see the star Hesperus, or Betelgeuse?

We've got to get them back, for they are the world our soul, our greater consciousness, lives in. The world of reason and science, the moon, a dead lump of earth, the sun, so much gas with spots: this is the dry and sterile little world the abstracted mind inhabits. The world of our little consciousness, which we know in our pettifogging *apartness*. This is how we know the world when we know it apart from ourselves, in the mean separateness of everything. When we know the world in togetherness with ourselves, we know the earth hyacinthine or Plutonic, we know the moon gives us our body as delight upon us, or steals it away, we know the purring of the great gold lion of the sun, who licks us like a lioness her cubs, making us bold, or else, like the red, angry lion, dashes at us with open claws. There are many ways of knowing, there are many sorts of knowledge. But the two ways of knowing, for man, are knowing in terms of apartness, which is mental, rational, scientific, and knowing in terms of togetherness, which is religious and poetic. The Christian religion lost, in Protestantism finally, the togetherness with the universe, the togetherness of the body, the sex, the emotions, the passions, with the earth and sun and stars.

But relationship is threefold. First, there is the relation to the living universe. Then comes the relation of man to woman. Then comes the relation of man to man. And each is a blood-relationship, not mere spirit or mind. We have abstracted the universe into Matter and Force, we have abstracted men and women into separate personalities — personalities being isolated units, incapable of togetherness — so that all three great relationships are bodiless, dead.

None, however, is quite so dead as the man-to-man relationship. I think, if we came to analyse to the last what men feel about one another today, we should find that every man feels every other man as a menace. It is a curious thing, but the more mental and ideal men are, the more they seem to feel the bodily presence of any other man a menace, a menace, as it were, to their very being. Every man that comes near me threatens my very existence: nay, more, my very being.

This is the ugly fact which underlies our civilization. As the advertisement of one of the war novels said, it is an epic of "friendship and hope, mud and blood," which means, of course, that the friendship and hope must end in mud and blood.

When the great crusade against sex and the body started in full blast with Plato, it was a crusade for "ideals," and for this "spiritual" knowledge in apartness. Sex is the great unifier. In its big, slower vibration it is the warmth of heart which makes people happy together, in togetherness. The idealist philosophies and religions set out deliberately to kill this. And they did it. Now they have done it. The last great ebullition of friendship and hope was squashed out in mud and blood. Now men are all separate little entities. While "kindness" is the glib order of the day — everybody *must* be "kind" — underneath this "kindness" we find a coldness of heart, a lack of heart, a callousness, that is very dreary. Every man *is* a menace to every other man.

Men only know one another in menace. Individualism has triumphed. If I am a sheer individual, then every other being, every other man especially, is over against me as a menace to me.

This is the peculiarity of our society today. We are all extremely sweet and "nice" to one another, because we merely fear one another.

The sense of isolation, followed by the sense of menace and of fear, is bound to arise as the feeling of oneness and community with our fellow men declines, and the feeling of individualism and personality, which is existence in isolation, increases. The so-called "cultured" classes are the first to develop "personality" and individualism, and the first to fall into this state of unconscious menace and fear. The working classes retain the old blood-warmth of oneness and togetherness some decades longer. Then they lose it too. And then class-consciousness becomes rampant, and class-hate. Class-hate and class-consciousness are only a sign that the old togetherness, the old blood-warmth has collapsed, and every man is really aware of himself in apartness. Then we have these hostile groupings of men for the sake of opposition, strife. Civil strife becomes a necessary condition of self-assertion.

This, again, is the tragedy of social life today. In the old England, the curious blood-connection held the classes together. The squires might be arrogant, violent, bullying, and unjust, yet in some ways they were *at one* with the people, part of the same blood-stream. We feel it in Defoe or Fielding. And then, in the mean Jane Austen, it is gone. Already this old maid typifies "personality" instead of character, the sharp knowing in apartness instead of knowing in togetherness, and she is, to my feeling, thoroughly unpleasant, English in the bad, mean, snobbish sense of the word, just as Fielding is English in the good, generous sense.

So, in *Lady Chatterley's Lover* we have a man, Sir Clifford, who is purely a personality, having lost entirely all connection with his fellow men and women, except those of usage. All warmth is gone entirely, the hearth is cold, the heart does not humanly exist. He is a pure product of our civilization, but he is the death of the great humanity of the world. He is kind by rule, but he does not know what warm sympathy means. He is what he is. And he loses the woman of his choice.

The other man still has the warmth of a man, but he is being hunted down, destroyed. Even it is a question if the woman who turns to him will really stand by him and his vital meaning.

I have been asked many times if I intentionally made Clifford paralysed, if it is symbolic. And literary friends say, it would have been better to have left him whole and potent, and to have made the woman leave him nevertheless.

As to whether the "symbolism" is intentional — I don't know.

Certainly not in the beginning, when Clifford was created. When I created Clifford and Connie, I had no idea what they were or why they were. They just came, pretty much as they are. But the novel was written, from start to finish, three times. And when I read the first version, I recognized that the lameness of Clifford was symbolic of the paralysis, the deeper emotional or passional paralysis, of most men of his sort and class today. I realized that it was perhaps taking an unfair advantage of Connie, to paralyse him technically. It made it so much more vulgar of her to leave him. Yet the story came as it did, by itself, so I left it alone. Whether we call it symbolism or not, it is, in the sense of its happening, inevitable.

And these notes, which I write now almost two years after the novel was finished, are not intended to explain or expound anything: only to give the emotional beliefs which perhaps are necessary as a background to the book. It is so obviously a book written in defiance of convention that perhaps some reason should be offered for the attitude of defiance: since the silly desire to *épater le bourgeois,* to bewilder the commonplace person, is not worth entertaining. If I use the taboo words, there is a reason. We shall never free the phallic reality from the "uplift" taint till we give it its own phallic language, and use the obscene words. The greatest blasphemy of all against the phallic reality is this "lifting it to a higher plane." Likewise, if the lady marries the gamekeeper — she hasn't done it yet — it is not class-spite, but in spite of class.

Finally, there are the correspondents who complain that I describe the pirated editions — some of them — but not the original. The original first edition, issued in Florence, is bound in hard covers, dullish mulberry-red paper with my phoenix (symbol of immortality, the bird rising new from the nest of flames) printed in black on the cover, and a white paper label on the back. The paper is good, creamy hand-rolled Italian paper, but the print, though nice, is ordinary, and the binding is just the usual binding of a little Florentine shop. There is no expert bookmaking in it: yet it is a pleasant volume, much more so than many far "superior" books.

And if there are many spelling errors — there are — it is because the book was set up in a little Italian printing shop, such a family affair, in which nobody knew one word of English. They none of them knew any English at all, so they were spared all blushes: and the proofs were terrible. The printer would do fairly well for a few pages, then he would go drunk, or something. And then the words danced weird and *macabre,* but not English. So that if still some of the hosts of errors exist, it is a mercy they are not more.

Then one paper wrote pitying the poor printer who was deceived into printing the book. Not deceived at all. A white-moustached little man who has just married a second wife, he was told: Now the book contains such-and-such words, in English, and it describes certain things. Don't you print it if you think it will get you into trouble! "What does it describe?" he asked. And when told, he said, with the short indifference of a Florentine: "O! *ma!* but we do it every day!" And it seemed, to him, to settle the matter entirely. Since it was nothing political or out of the way, there was nothing to think about. Every-day concerns, commonplace.

But it was a struggle, and the wonder is the book came out as well as it did. There was just enough type to set up a half of it: so the half was set up, the thousand copies were printed and, as a measure of caution, the two hundred on ordinary paper, the little second edition, as well: then the type was distributed, and the second half set up.

Then came the struggle of delivery. The book was stopped by the American customs almost at once. Fortunately in England there was a delay. So that practically the whole edition — at least eight hundred copies, surely — must have gone to England.

Then came the storms of vulgar vituperation. But they were inevitable. "But we do it every day," says a little Italian printer. "Monstrous and horrible!" shrieks a section of the British press. "Thank you for a really sexual book about sex, at last. I am so tired of a-sexual books," says one of the most distinguished citizens of Florence to me — an Italian. "I don't know — I don't know — if it's not a bit too strong," says a timid Florentine critic — an Italian. "Listen, Signor Lawrence, you find it really necessary to *say* it?" I told him I did, and he pondered. "Well, one of them was a brainy vamp, and the other was a sexual moron," said an American woman, referring to the two men in the book — "so I'm afraid Connie had a poor choice — *as usual!*"

APPENDIX

United States District Court

SOUTHERN DISTRICT OF NEW YORK

GROVE PRESS, INC. and READERS'
SUBSCRIPTION, INC.,

Plaintiffs,

— against —

ROBERT K. CHRISTENBERRY, individually and as Postmaster of the City of New York,

Defendant.

Civil 147–87

OPINION

BRYAN, *District Judge:*

These two actions against the Postmaster of New York, now con-
solidated, arise out of the denial of the United States mails to the recently published Grove Press unexpurgated edition of "Lady Chatterley's Lover" by D. H. Lawrence.

Plaintiffs seek to restrain the Postmaster from enforcing a decision
of the Post Office Department that the unexpurgated "Lady Chatterley's
Lover," and circulars announcing its availability, are non-mailable under
the statute barring obscene matter from the mails (18 U. S. C. § 1461).[1]
They also seek a declaratory judgment to the effect (1) that the novel is
not "obscene, lewd, lascivious, indecent or filthy" in content or character, and is not non-mailable under the statute or, in the alternative, (2)
that if the novel be held to fall within the purview of the statute, the
statute is to that extent invalid and violates plaintiffs' rights in contravention of the First and Fifth Amendments.

Grove Press, Inc., one of the plaintiffs, is the publisher of the book.
Readers' Subscription, Inc., the other plaintiff, is a book club which has
rights to distribute it.

---

[1] The relevant portions of § 1461 provide:

"Every obscene, lewd, lascivious, indecent, filthy or vile article * * * and
"Every written or printed * * * circular, * * * or notice of any kind giving information * * * where, or how, or from whom * * * any of such
* * * articles * * * may be obtained * * *

"Is declared to be nonmailable matter and shall not be conveyed in the
mails or delivered from any post office or by any letter carrier."

The statute provides penalties for violation of up to five years imprisonment and
a maximum fine of $5,000 for a first offense and up to ten years' imprisonment and
a maximum $10,000 fine for subsequent offenses.

Defendant has moved and plaintiffs have cross-moved for summary judgment, pursuant to Rule 56, F. R. C. P. There are no disputed issues of fact. The cases are before me for final determination on the pleadings, the decision of the Postmaster General, the record before him and supplemental affidavits.[2]

On April 30, 1959 the New York Postmaster withheld from dispatch some 20,000 copies of circulars deposited for mailing by Readers' Subscription, which announced the availability of the new Grove edition of Lady Chatterley. At about the same time he also detained a number of copies of the book which had been deposited for mailing by Grove Press.

On May 8, 1959 letters of complaint issued by the General Counsel of the Post Office Department were served on Grove and Readers' Subscription alleging that there was probable cause to believe that these mailings violated 18 U. S. C. § 1461, and advising them of a departmental hearing. The respondents filed answers denying these allegations and a hearing was held before the Judicial Officer of the Post Office Department on May 14, 1959.[3]

The General Counsel, as complainant, introduced the Grove edition and the circulars which had been detained and rested.

The respondents offered (1) testimony as to their reputation and standing in the book publishing and distribution fields and their purpose in publishing and distributing the novel; (2) reviews of the book in leading newspapers and literary periodicals throughout the country; (3) copies of editorials and comments in leading newspapers concerning publication of the book and its anticipated impact; (4) news articles dealing with the banning of the book by the Post Office; and (5) expert testimony by two leading literary critics, Malcolm Cowley and Alfred Kazin, as to the literary stature of the work and its author, contemporary acceptance of literature dealing with sex and sex relations and their own opinions as to the effect of the book on its readers. The editorials and comments and the news articles were excluded.

The Judicial Officer before whom the hearing was held did not decide the issues. On May 28 he issued an order referring the proceedings to the Postmaster General "for final departmental decision." [4]

---

[2] Plaintiffs originally moved for a preliminary injunction but that motion is moot in the present posture of the case.

[3] The Judicial Officer heard the case pursuant to a stipulation between the parties which had the effect of obviating the requirement that the case be heard by an independent Hearing Examiner. See *Borg-Johnson Electronics, Inc.* v. *Christenberry*, D. C. S. D. N. Y., 169 F. Supp. 746.

[4] This referral was made pursuant to paragraph III (b) 23 F. R. 2817, which provides certain "Decisions and orders of the Judicial Officer * * * shall be the final departmental decision * * * except that the Judicial Officer may refer any proceeding to * * * the Postmaster General * * * for final decision." The order of the Judicial Officer making the referral said:

"The complainant alleges that the book 'Lady Chatterley's Lover' is obscene and nonmailable under 18 U. S. C. 1461 and that the circular of Readers' Subscription, Inc. gives information as to where obscenity may be obtained. The

On June 11, 1959 the Postmaster General rendered a departmental decision finding that the Grove edition "is obscene and non-mailable pursuant to 18 U. S. Code § 1461," and that the Readers' Subscription circulars "give information where obscene material, namely, the book in issue in this case, may be obtained and are non-mailable * * *."

This litigation, which had been commenced prior to the decision, was then brought on for hearing.

I

The basic question here is whether the unexpurgated "Lady Chatterley's Lover" is obscene within the meaning of 18 U. S. C. § 1461,[5] and is thus excluded from the protections afforded freedom of speech and the press by the First Amendment.

However, the defendant takes the position that this question is not before me for decision. He urges that the determination by the Postmaster General that this novel is obscene and non-mailable is conclusive upon the court unless it is found to be unsupported by substantial evidence and is clearly wrong. He argues, therefore, that I may not determine the issue of obscenity *de novo*.

Thus, an initial question is raised as to the scope of the court's power of review. In the light of the issues presented, the basis of the Postmaster General's decision, and the record before him, this question is not of substance.

(1) Prior to *Roth* v. *United States,* 354 U. S. 476, the Supreme Court had "always assumed that obscenity is not protected by the freedoms of speech and press." However, until then the constitutional question had not been directly passed upon by the court. In *Roth* the question was squarely posed.

The court held, in accord with its long-standing assumption, that "obscenity is not within the area of constitutionally protected speech or press." [6]

The court was faced with a dilemma. On the one hand it was required to eschew any impingement upon the cherished freedoms of speech and the press guaranteed by the Constitution and so essential to a free society. On the other hand it was faced with the recognized social evil presented by the purveyance of pornography.

---

complainant admits that the novel has literary merit but claims that the obscene passages outweigh the literary merit.

"The book at issue, which is the unexpurgated version, has for many years been held to be nonmailable by the Post Office Department and non-importable by the Bureau of Customs of the Department of the Treasury. To hold the book to be mailable matter would require a reversal of rulings of long standing by this Department and to cast doubt on the rulings of a coordinate executive department."

[5] I use the word "obscene" as covering the words "obscene, lewd, lascivious, indecent, filthy or vile" as used in the statute in so far as they may be applicable to this book.

[6] The court expressly limited its grant of certiorari to constitutional questions concerning the validity of Section 1461 on its face, and thus was not concerned with the specific facts of the case. *Roth* v. *United States,* 352 U. S. 964.

The opinion of Mr. Justice Brennan for the majority makes it plain that the area which can be excluded from constitutional protection without impinging upon the free speech and free press guarantees is narrowly limited. He says (p. 484):

"All ideas having even the slightest redeeming social importance — unorthodox ideas, controversial ideas, even ideas hateful to the prevailing climate of opinion — have the full protection of the guarantees, unless excludable because they encroach upon the limited area of more important interests."

He gives stern warning that no publication advancing such ideas can be suppressed under the guise of regulation of public morals or censorship of public reading matter. As he says (p. 488):

"The fundamental freedoms of speech and press have contributed greatly to the development and well-being of our free society and are indispensable to its continued growth. Ceaseless vigilance is the watchword to prevent their erosion by Congress or by the States. The door barring federal and state intrusion into this area cannot be left ajar; it must be kept tightly closed and opened only the slightest crack necessary to prevent encroachment upon more important interests."

It was against these constitutional requirements that the Court laid down general standards for judging obscenity, recognizing that it was "vital that [such] standards * * * safeguard the protection of freedom of speech and press for material which does not treat sex" in an obscene manner. The standards were "whether to the average person, applying contemporary community standards, the dominant theme of the material taken as a whole appeals to prurient interest."

The Court did not attempt to apply these standards to a specific set of facts. It merely circumscribed and limited the excluded area in general terms.

Plainly application of these standards to specific material may involve no little difficulty as the court was well aware. Cases involving "hard core" pornography, or what Judge Woolsey referred to as "dirt for dirt's sake,"[7] purveyed furtively by dealers in smut, are relatively simple. But works of literary merit present quite a different problem, and one which the majority in *Roth* did not reach as such.[8]

Chief Justice Warren, concurring in the result, said of this problem (354 U. S. p. 476):

"* * * The history of the application of laws designed to suppress the obscene demonstrates convincingly that the power of govern-

---

[7] *United States* v. *One Book Called "Ulysses,"* D. C. S. D. N. Y., 5 F. Supp. 182, aff'd, 2 Cir., 72 F. 2d 705.

[8] "No issue is presented * * * concerning the obscenity of the material involved." (Footnote 8, p. 481.)

ment can be invoked under them against great art or literature, scientific treatises, or works exciting social controversy. Mistakes of the past prove that there is a strong countervailing interest to be considered in the freedoms guaranteed by the First and Fourteenth Amendments."

And Mr. Justice Harlan, dissenting, also deeply concerned, had this to say (pp. 497, 498):

"* * * The suppression of a particular writing or other tangible form of expression is * * * an *individual* matter, and in the nature of things every such suppression raises an individual constitutional problem, in which a reviewing court must determine for *itself* whether the attacked expression is suppressible within constitutional standards. Since those standards do not readily lend themselves to generalized definitions, the constitutional problem in the last analysis becomes one of particularized judgments which appellate courts must make for themselves.

"I do not think that reviewing courts can escape this responsibility by saying that the trier of the facts, be it a jury or a judge, has labeled the questioned matter as 'obscene,' for, if 'obscenity' is to be suppressed, the question whether a particular work is of that character involves not really an issue of fact but a question of constitutional *judgment* of the most sensitive and delicate kind."

Mr. Justice Frankfurter, concurring in *Kingsley International Pictures Corp.* v. *Regents,* decided on June 29, 1959, 27 L. W. 4492, expressed a similar view. He pointed out that in determining whether particular works are entitled to the constitutional protections of freedom of expression "We cannot escape such instance by instance, case by case * * * [constitutional adjudication] in all the variety of situations that come before this Court." And Mr. Justice Harlan, in the same case, also concurring in the result, speaks of "the necessity for individualized adjudication. In the very nature of things the problems in this area are ones of individual cases * * *."

These views are not inconsistent with the decisions of the majority determining both *Roth* and *Kingsley* upon *broader* constitutional grounds.

It would seem that the Court itself made such "individualized" or "case by case" adjudications as to the obscenity of specific material in at least two cases following *Roth.* In *One, Inc.* v. *Olesen,* 355 U. S. 371 and *Sunshine Book Co.* v. *Summerfield,* 355 U. S. 372, the courts below had found in no uncertain terms that the material was obscene within the meaning of Section 1461.[9] In each case the Supreme Court in a one sentence per curiam opinion granted certiorari and reversed on the authority of *Roth.*

One, Inc. v. *Olesen,* and *Sunshine Book Co.* v. *Summerfield,* involved

---

[9] *One, Inc.* v. *Olesen,* 9 Cir., 241 F. 2d 772; *Sunshine Book Co.* v. *Summerfield,* D. C. D. C., 128 F. Supp. 564, D. C. Cir., 249 F. 2d 114.

determinations by the Post Office barring material from the mails on the ground that it was obscene. In both the District Court had found that the publication was obscene and that the determination of the Post Office should be upheld. In both the Court of Appeals had affirmed the findings of the District Court.

Yet in each the Supreme Court, without discussion, summarily reversed on the authority of *Roth*. As Judge Desmond of the New York Court of Appeals said of these cases — "Presumably, the court having looked at those books simply held them not to be obscene." [10]

It is no less the duty of this court in the case at bar to scrutinize the book with great care and to determine for itself whether it is within the constitutional protections afforded by the First Amendment, or whether it may be excluded from those protections because it is obscene under the *Roth* tests.

(2) Such review is quite consistent with the Administrative Procedure Act (5 U. S. C. § 1001, et seq.), assuming that the act is applicable here.

This is not a case where the agency determination under review is dependent on "a fair estimate of the worth of the testimony of witnesses or its informed judgment on matters within its special competence or both." See *Universal Camera Corp.* v. *Labor Board*, 340 U. S. 474, 490. *Cf. O'Leary* v. *Brown-Pacific-Maxon*, 340 U. S. 504; *Gooding* v. *Willard*, 2 Cir., 209 F. 2d 913.

There were no disputed facts before the Postmaster General. The facts as to the mailings and the detainer were stipulated and the only issue before him was whether "Lady Chatterley's Lover" was obscene. The complainant relied on the text of the novel and nothing more to establish obscenity. Respondents' evidence was wholly uncontradicted, and, except for the opinions of the critics Cowley and Kazin as to the effect of the book upon its readers, it scarcely could have been. The complainant conceded that the book had literary merit. The views of the critics as to the place of the novel and its author in twentieth century English literature have not been questioned.

As the Postmaster General said, he attempted to apply to the book "the tests which, it is my understanding, the courts have established for determining questions of obscenity." Thus, all he did was to apply the statute, as he interpreted it in the light of the decisions, to the book. His interpretation and application of the statute involved quesions of law, not questions of fact.

The Postmaster General has no special competence or technical knowledge on this subject which qualifies him to render an informed judgment entitled to special weight in the courts. There is no parallel here to determinations of such agencies as the Interstate Commerce Commission, the Securities and Exchange Commission, the National Labor Relations Board, the Federal Communications Commission, the Federal Power Commission, or many others on highly technical and

---

[10] Concurring in *Matter of Kingsley Corp.* v. *Regents*, 4 N. Y. 2d 349, 368.

complicated subject matter upon which they have specialized knowledge and are particularly qualified to speak.

No doubt the Postmaster General has similar qualifications on many questions involving the administration of the Post Office Department, the handling of the mails, postal rates and other matters. See *Bates & Guild Co.* v. *Payne,* 194 U. S. 106. But he has no special competence to determine what constitutes obscenity within the meaning of Section 1461, or that "contemporary community standards are not such that this book should be allowed to be transmitted in the mails" or that the literary merit of the book is outweighed by its pornographic features, as he found. Such questions involve interpretation of a statute, which also imposes criminal penalties, and its application to the allegedly offending material. The determination of such questions is peculiarly for the courts, particularly in the light of the constitutional questions implicit in each case.[11]

It has been suggested that the court cannot interfere with the order of the Postmaster General unless it finds that he abused his discretion. But it does not appear that the Postmaster General has been vested with "discretion" finally to determine whether a book is obscene within the meaning of the statute.

It is unnecessary to pass on the questions posed by the plaintiffs as to whether the Postmaster General has any power to impose prior restraints upon the mailing of matter allegedly obscene and whether the enforcement of the statute is limited to criminal proceedings, though it seems to me that these questions are not free from doubt.[12]

Assuming power in the Postmaster General to withhold obscene matter from dispatch in the mails temporarily, a grant of discretion to make a final determination as to whether a book is obscene and should be denied to the public should certainly not be inferred in the absence of a clear and direct mandate. As the Supreme Court pointed out under comparable circumstances in *Hannegan* v. *Esquire, Inc.,* 327 U. S. 146, 151, to vest such power in the Postmaster General would, in effect, give him the power of censorship and that "is so abhorrent to our traditions that a purpose to grant it should not be easily inferred."

No such grant of power to the Postmaster General has been called

---

[11] Professor Davis notes in *Administrative Law Treatise* (1958), Vol. 4, § 30.07, "Substitution of judicial for administrative judgment is often rather clearly desirable, * * * [on questions] which (1) transcend the single field of the particular agency, (2) call for interpretation of the common law, * * * (4) are affected substantially by constitutional considerations, whether or not a constitutional issue is directly presented, * * * (6) bring into question judge-made law previously developed in the course of statutory interpretation * * *." These criteria are all present here.

[12] These questions have never been decided by the Supreme Court. The sharply divided Court of Appeals for the District of Columbia Circuit, sitting *en banc* found that the Postmaster General had such power in *Sunshine Book Co.* v. *Summerfield, supra.* But I find the dissenting opinion persuasive.

to my attention and I have found none.[13] Whatever administrative functions the Postmaster General has go no further than closing the mails to material which is obscene within the meaning of the statute. This is not an area in which the Postmaster General has any "discretion" which is entitled to be given special weight by the courts.[14]

The Administrative Procedure Act makes the reviewing court responsible for determining all relevant questions of law, for interpreting and applying all constitutional and statutory provisions and for setting aside agency action not in accordance with law. (5 U. S. C. § 1009.) The question presented here falls within this framework.

Thus, the question presented for decision is whether "Lady Chatterley's Lover" is obscene within the meaning of the statute and thus excludable from constitutional protections. I will now consider that question.

II

This unexpurgated edition of "Lady Chatterley's Lover" has never before been published either in the United States or England, though comparatively small editions were published by Lawrence himself in Italy and authorized for publication in France, and a number of pirated copies found their way to this country.

Grove Press is a reputable publisher with a good list which includes a number of distinguished writers and serious works. Before publishing this edition Grove consulted recognized literary critics and authorities on English literature as to the advisability of publication. All were of the view that the work was of major literary importance and should be made available to the American public.

No one is naive enough to think that Grove Press did not expect to profit from the book. Nevertheless the format and composition of the volume, the advertising and promotional material and the whole approach to publication, treat the book as a serious work of literature. The book is distributed through leading bookstores throughout the country. There has been no attempt by the publisher to appeal to prurience or the prurient minded.

The Grove edition has a preface by Archibald MacLeish, former Librarian of Congress, Pulitzer Prize winner, and one of this country's

---

[13] Even under 39 U. S. C. § § 259a and 259b, which give the Postmaster General power to withhold incoming mail from a purveyor of obscenity "upon evidence satisfactory" to him, an application to the District Court is required within twenty days for a determination, inter alia, as to whether the detention is reasonable or necessary. This is in contrast to Section 1461, included in the Criminal Code, where no such statutory scheme is provided.

[14] The defendant cites language to indicate that the question of whether material is obscene is committed to agency discretion. One line of cases deals with "fraud orders." (39 U. S. C. § 259.) Fraud is almost always a question of fact and Section 259 provides that the Postmaster General may deny the mails "upon evidence satisfactory to him." Such cases as *Gottlieb* v. *Schaffer*, D. C. S. D. N. Y., 141 F.

most distinguished poets and literary figures, giving his appraisal of the novel. There follows an introduction by Mark Schorer, Professor of English Literature at the University of California, a leading scholar of D. H. Lawrence and his work. The introduction is a critique of the novel against the background of Lawrence's life, work and philosophy. At the end of the novel there is a biographical note as to the circumstances under which it was written and first published. Thus, the novel is placed in a setting which emphasizes its literary qualities and its place as a significant work of a major English novelist.

Readers' Subscription has handled the book in the same vein. The relatively small number of Readers' Subscription subscribers is composed largely of people in academic, literary and scholarly fields. Its list of books includes works of high literary merit, including books by and about D. H. Lawrence.

There is nothing of "the leer of the sensualist" [15] in the promotion or methods of distribution of this book. There is no suggestion of any attempt to pander to the lewd and lascivious minded for profit. The facts are all to the contrary.

Publication met with unanimous critical approval. The book was favorably received by the literary critics of such diverse publications as the New York Times, the Chicago Tribune, the San Francisco Call Bulletin, the New York Post, the New York Herald Tribune, Harpers and Time, to mention only some. The critics were not agreed upon their appraisal. Critical comment ranged from acclaim on the one hand to more restrained views that this was not the best of Lawrence's writing, and was dated and in parts "wooden." But as MacLeish says in the preface,

> "* * * in spite of these reservations no responsible critic would deny the book a place as one of the most important works of fiction of the century, and no reader of any kind could undertake to express an opinion about the literature of the time or about

---

Supp. 7, which apply the substantial evidence test to agency findings of fact under these circumstances are clearly distinguishable. See, also, *Donaldson* v. *Read Magazine, Inc.*, 333 U. S. 178.

Other cases cited deal with matters requiring expert judgment in the administration of the mails. E.g., *Smith* v. *Hitchcock*, 226 U. S. 53.

Cases cited involving obscenity while referring to "administrative discretion" considered the facts. In *Bowery Enterprises* v. *Christenberry*, Civ. 140-233, D. C. S. D. N. Y., 1958, Judge Dimock found the material clearly obscene. It was "unnecessary to seek support in the rule that an administrative determination must stand unless clearly wrong." In *Anderson* v. *Patten*, D. C. S. D. N. Y., 247 Fed. 382, the material, the subject matter and the treatment were salacious. In *Roth* v. *Goldman*, 2 Cir., 172 F. 2d 788, the materials had "little excuse for being beyond their provocative obscenity * * *."

Monart, Inc. v. *Christenberry*, D. C. S. D. N. Y., 168 F. Supp. 654, was concerned only with the power of the Post Office.

These cases do not hold that a Post Office determination of obscenity is entitled to special weight.

[15] Woolsey, *D. J.* in *United States* v. *One Book Called "Ulysses," supra.*

the spiritual history that literature expresses without making his peace in one way or another with D. H. Lawrence and with this work."

Publication of the Grove edition was a major literary event. It was greeted by editorials in leading newspapers throughout the country unanimously approving the publication and viewing with alarm possible attempts to ban the book.

It was against this background that the New York Postmaster impounded the book and the Postmaster General barred it. The decision of the Postmaster General, in a brief four pages, relied on three cases, *Roth* v. *United States, supra, United States* v. *One Book Called "Ulysses,"* D. C. S. D. N. Y., 5 F. Supp. 182, aff'd, 2 Cir., 72 F. 2d 705, and *Besig* v. *United States,* 9 Cir., 208 F. 2d 142. While he quotes from *Roth* the Postmaster General relies principally on *Besig,* which was not reviewed by the Supreme Court. It may be noted that the Ninth Circuit relied heavily on *Besig* in *One, Inc.* v. *Olesen, supra,* which was summarily reversed by the Supreme Court on the authority of *Roth.*

He refers to the book as "currently withheld from the mails in the United States and barred from the mails by several other major nations." His only discussion of its content is as follows:

"The contemporary community standards are not such that this book should be allowed to be transmitted in the mails.

"The book is replete with descriptions in minute detail of sexual acts engaged in or discussed by the book's principal characters. These descriptions utilize filthy, offensive and degrading words and terms. Any literary merit the book may have is far outweighed by the pornographic and smutty passages and words, so that the book, taken as a whole, is an obscene and filthy work.

"I therefore see no need to modify or reverse the prior rulings of this Department and the Department of the Treasury with respect to this edition of this book." [16]

This seems to be the first time since the notable opinions of Judge Woolsey and Judge Augustus Hand in *United States* v. *One Book Called "Ulysses," supra,* in 1934 that a book of comparable literary stature has come before the federal courts charged with violating the federal obscenity statutes. That case held that James Joyce's "Ulysses" which had been seized by the Customs under Section 305 of the Tariff

---

[16] The "rulings" referred to, apparently made even before the *Ulysses* case, were not produced at the hearing and it does not appear that they have ever seen the light of day. There is nothing in the record as to their content, the grounds on which they were based, whether whatever parties may have been involved were given a hearing, or what standards were applied. Nor is there any indication as to what "major nations" have banned the book or whether in such countries there are any constitutional or other legal protections afforded speech and press.

Act of 1930 was not obscene within the meaning of that statute. It thoroughly discussed the standards to be applied in determining this question.

The essence of the *Ulysses* holding is that a work of literary merit is not obscene under federal law merely because it contains passages and language dealing with sex in a most candid and realistic fashion and uses many four-letter Anglo-Saxon words. Where a book is written with honesty and seriousness of purpose, and the portions which might be considered obscene are relevant to the theme, it is not condemned by the statute even though "it justly may offend many." "Ulysses" contains numerous passages dealing very frankly with sex and the sex act and is free in its use of four-letter Anglo-Saxon words. Yet both Judge Woolsey in the District Court, and Judge Hand in the Court of Appeals, found that it was a sincere and honest book which was not in any sense "dirt for dirt's sake." [17] They both concluded that "Ulysses" was a work of high literary merit, written by a gifted and serious writer, which did not have the dominant effect of promoting lust or prurience and therefore did not fall within the interdiction of the statute.

Roth v. *United States, supra,* decided by the Supreme Court in 1957, twenty-three years later, unlike the *Ulysses* case, did not deal with the application of the obscenity statutes to specific material. It laid down general tests circumscribing the area in which matter is excludable from constitutional protections because it is obscene, so as to avoid impingement on First Amendment guarantees.[18]

The court distilled from the prior cases (including the *Ulysses* case, which it cited with approval) the standards to be applied [19] — "whether to the average person, applying contemporary community standards, the dominant theme of the material taken as a whole appeals to prurient interest."

The court saw no significant difference between this expression of the standards and those in the American Law Institute Model Penal Code[20] to the effect that

> "* * * A thing is obscene if, considered as a whole, its predominant appeal is to prurient interest, i.e., a shameful or morbid interest in nudity, sex, or excretion, and if it goes substantially beyond

---

[17] As Judge Woolsey said (5 F. Supp. p. 184): "Each word of the book contributes like a bit of mosaic to the detail of the picture which Joyce is seeking to construct for his readers."

[18] There was no question but that the material involved in *Roth* was hard core pornography and that the defendants were engaged "in the commercial exploitation of the morbid and shameful craving for materials with prurient effect." (354 U. S., p. 496.)

[19] For a comprehensive review of the prior material see Judge Frank's provocative concurring opinion in the Court of Appeals which points to problems in this field still unresolved. *United States* v. *Roth,* 2 Cir., 237 F. 2d 796, 801.

[20] § 207.10(2), Tent. Draft No. 6, 1957.

customary limits of candor in description or representation of such matters * * *."

These standards are not materially different from those applied in *Ulysses* to the literary work considered there. Since the *Roth* case dealt with these standards for judging obscenity in general terms and the *Ulysses* case dealt with application of such standards to a work of recognized literary stature, the two should be read together.

A number of factors are involved in the application of these tests.

As Mr. Justice Brennan pointed out in *Roth,* sex and obscenity are by no means synonymous and "[t]he portrayal of sex, e.g., in art, literature and scientific works, is not in itself sufficient reason to deny material the constitutional protection of freedom of speech and press." As he said, sex has been "a subject of absorbing interest to mankind through the ages; it is one of the vital problems of human interest and public concern." The subject may be discussed publicly and truthfully without previous restraint or fear of subsequent punishment as long as it does not fall within the narrowly circumscribed interdicted area.

Both cases held that, to be obscene, the dominant effect of the book must be an appeal to prurient interest — that is to say, shameful or morbid interest in sex. Such a theme must so predominate as to submerge any ideas of "redeeming social importance" which the publication contains.

It is not the effect upon the irresponsible, the immature or the sensually minded which is controlling. The material must be judged in terms of its effect on those it is likely to reach who are conceived of as the average man of normal sensual impulses,[21] or, as Judge Woolsey says, "what the French would call l'homme moyen sensuel."

The material must also exceed the limits of tolerance imposed by current standards of the community with respect to freedom of expression in matters concerning sex and sex relations. Moreover, a book is not to be judged by excerpts or individual passages but must be judged as a whole.

All of these factors must be present before a book can be held obscene and thus outside constitutional protections.

Judged by these standards, "Lady Chatterley's Lover" is not obscene. The decision of the Postmaster General that it is obscene and therefore non-mailable is contrary to law and clearly erroneous. This is emphasized when the book is considered against its background and in the light of its stature as a significant work of a distinguished English novelist.

D. H. Lawrence is one of the most important novelists writing in the English language in this century. Whether he is, as some authorities say, the greatest English novelist since Joseph Conrad, or one of a number of major figures, makes little difference. He was a writer of great gifts and of undoubted artistic integrity.

---

[21] See *Volanski* v. *United States*, 6 Cir., 246 F. 2d 842.

The text of this edition of "Lady Chatterley's Lover" was written by Lawrence toward the close of his life and was his third version of the novel, originally called "Tenderness."

The book is almost as much a polemic as a novel.

In it Lawrence was expressing his deep and bitter dissatisfaction with what he believed were the stultifying effects of advancing industrialization and his own somewhat obscure philosophic remedy of a return to "naturalness." He attacks what he considered to be the evil effects of industrialization upon the wholesome and natural life of all classes in England. In his view this was having disastrous consequences on English society and on the English countryside. It had resulted in devitalization of the upper classes of society and debasement of the lower classes. One result, as he saw it, was the corrosion of both the emotional and physical sides of man as expressed in his sexual relationships which had become increasingly artificial and unwholesome.

The novel develops the contrasts and conflicts in characters under these influences.

The plot is relatively simple.

Constance Chatterley is married to a baronet, returned from the first World War paralyzed from the waist down. She is physically frustrated and dissatisfied with the artificiality and sterility of her life and of the society in which she moves. Her husband, immersed in himself, seeks compensation for his own frustrations in the writing of superficial and brittle fiction and in the exploitation of his coal mining properties, a symbol of the creeping industrial blight. Failing to find satisfaction in an affair with a man in her husband's circle, Constance Chatterley finds herself increasingly restless and unhappy. Her husband half-heartedly urges her to have a child by another man whom he will treat as his heir. Repelled by the suggestion that she casually beget a child, she is drawn to Mellors, the gamekeeper, sprung from the working class who, having achieved a measure of spiritual and intellectual independence, is a prototype of Lawrence's natural man. They establish a deeply passionate and tender relationship which is described at length and in detail. At the conclusion she is pregnant and plans to obtain a divorce and marry the gamekeeper.

This plot serves as a vehicle through which Lawrence develops his basic theme of contrast between his own philosophy and the sterile and debased society which he attacks. Most of the characters are prototypes. The plot and theme are meticulously worked out with honesty and sincerity.

The book is replete with fine writing and with descriptive passages of rare beauty. There is no doubt of its literary merit.

It contains a number of passages describing sexual intercourse in great detail with complete candor and realism. Four-letter Anglo-Saxon words are used with some frequency.

These passages and this language understandably will shock the sensitive minded. Be that as it may, these passages are relevant to the plot and to the development of the characters and of their lives as Lawrence unfolds them. The language which shocks, except in a rare instance or two, is not inconsistent with character, situation or theme.

Even if it be assumed that these passages and this language taken in isolation tend to arouse shameful, morbid and lustful sexual desires in the average reader, they are an integral, and to the author a necessary[22] part of the development of theme, plot and character. The dominant theme, purpose and effect of the book as a whole is not an appeal to prurience or the prurient minded. The book is not "dirt for dirt's sake." [23] Nor do these passages and this language submerge the dominant theme so as to make the book obscene even if they could be considered and found to be obscene in isolation.

What the Postmaster General seems to have done is precisely what the Supreme Court in *Roth* and the courts in the *Ulysses* case said ought not to be done. He has lifted from the novel individual passages and language, found them to be obscene in isolation and therefore condemned the book as a whole. He has disregarded the dominant theme and effect of the book and has read these passages and this language as if they were separable and could be taken out of context. Thus he has "weighed" the isolated passages which he considered obscene against the remainder of the book and concluded that the work as a whole must be condemned.

Writing about sex is not in itself pornographic, as the Postmaster General recognized. Nor does the fact that sex is a major theme of a book condemn the book as obscene. Neither does the use of "four letter" words, despite the offense they may give. "Ulysses" was found not to be obscene despite long passages containing similar descriptions and language. As Judge Woolsey said there (5 F. Supp. pp. 183, 184):

> "The words which are criticized as dirty are old Saxon words known to almost all men and, I venture, to many women, and are such words as would be naturally and habitually used, I believe, by

---

[22] See D. H. Lawrence, "Sex, Literature, and Censorship" (Twayne Publishers, 1953), p. 89. Essay "A Propros of *Lady Chatterly's Lover*."

[23] As Mr. Justice Frankfurter pointed out in *Kingsley International Pictures Corp. v. Regents, supra,* Lawrence

> "knew there was such a thing as pornography, dirt for dirt's sake, or, to be more accurate, dirt for money's sake. This is what D. H. Lawrence wrote:

> " 'But even I would censor genuine pornography, rigorously. It would not be very difficult. In the first place, genuine pornography is almost always underworld, it doesn't come into the open. In the second, you can recognize it by the insult it offers invariably, to sex, and to the human spirit.

> " 'Pornography is the attempt to insult sex, to do dirt on it. This is unpardonable. Take the very lowest instance, the picture post-card sold underhand, by the underworld, in most cities. What I have seen of them have been of an ugliness to make you cry. The insult to the human body, the insult to a vital human relationship! Ugly and cheap they make the human nudity, ugly and degraded they make the sexual act, trivial and cheap and nasty.'
> (D. H. Lawrence, Pornography and Obscenity, p. 13.) (Collected in Lawrence, "Sex, Literature, and Censorship," *supra,* p. 69.)

the types of folk whose life, physical and mental, Joyce is seeking to describe."

Such words "are, almost without exception, of honest Anglo-Saxon ancestry and were not invented for purely scatological effect." [24]

The tests of obscenity are not whether the book or passages from it are in bad taste or shock or offend the sensibilities of an individual, or even of a substantial segment of the community. Nor are we concerned with whether the community would approve of Constance Chatterley's morals. The statute does not purport to regulate the morals portrayed or the ideas expressed in a novel, whether or not they are contrary to the accepted moral code, nor could it constitutionally do so. *Kingsley International Pictures* v. *Regents, supra.*

Plainly "Lady Chatterley's Lover" is offensive to the Postmaster General, and I respect his personal views. As a matter of personal opinion I disagree with him for I do not personally find the book offensive.

But the personal views of neither of us are controlling here. The standards for determining what constitutes obscenity under this statute have been laid down. These standards must be objectively applied regardless of personal predilections.

There has been much discussion of the intent and purpose of Lawrence in writing Lady Chatterley. It is suggested that the intent and purpose of the author has no relevance to the question as to whether his work is obscene and must be disregarded.

No doubt an author may write a clearly obscene book in the mistaken belief that he is serving a high moral purpose. The fact that this is the author's purpose does not redeem the book from obscenity.

But the sincerity and honesty of purpose of an author as expressed in the manner in which a book is written and in which his theme and ideas are developed has a great deal to do with whether it is of literary and intellectual merit. Here, as in the *Ulysses* case, there is no question about Lawrence's honesty and sincerity of purpose, artistic integrity and lack of intention to appeal to prurient interest.

Thus, this is an honest and sincere novel of literary merit and its dominant theme and effect, taken as a whole, is not an appeal to the prurient interest of the average reader.

This would seem to end the matter. However, the Postmaster General's finding that the book is non-mailable because it offends contemporary community standards bears some discussion.

I am unable to ascertain upon what the Postmaster General based this conclusion. The record before him indicates general acceptance of the book throughout the country and nothing was shown to the contrary. The critics were unanimous. Editorial comment by leading journals of opinion welcomed the publication and decried any attempts to ban it.

---

[24] Judge Bok in *Commonwealth* v. *Gordon,* 66 D. & C. Rep. (Pa.) 101, 114.

It is true that the editorial comment was excluded by the Judicial Officer at the hearing. But it seems to me that this was error. These expressions were relevant and material on the question of whether the book exceeded the limits of freedom of expression in matters involving sex and sex relations tolerated by the community at large in these times.

The contemporary standards of the community and the limits of its tolerance cannot be measured or ascertained accurately. There is no poll available to determine such questions. Surely expressions by leading newspapers, with circulations of millions, are some evidence at least as to what the limits of tolerance by present day community standards are, if we must embark upon a journey of exploration into such uncharted territory.

Quite apart from this, the broadening of freedom of expression and of the frankness with which sex and sex relations are dealt with at the present time require no discussion. In one best selling novel after another frank descriptions of the sex act and "four-letter" words appear with frequency. These trends appear in all media of public expression, in the kind of language used and the subjects discussed in polite society, in pictures, advertisements and dress, and in other ways familiar to all. Much of what is now accepted would have shocked the community to the core a generation ago. Today such things are generally tolerated whether we approve or not.

I hold that, at this stage in the development of our society, this major English novel does not exceed the outer limits of the tolerance which the community as a whole gives to writing about sex and sex relations.

One final word about the constitutional problem implicit here.

It is essential to the maintenance of a free society that the severest restrictions be placed upon restraints which may tend to prevent the dissemination of ideas.[25] It matters not whether such ideas be expressed in political pamphlets or works of political, economic or social theory or criticism, or through artistic media. All such expressions must be freely available.

A work of literature published and distributed through normal channels by a reputable publisher stands on quite a different footing from hard core pornography furtively sold for the purpose of profiting by the titillation of the dirty minded. The courts have been deeply and properly concerned about the use of obscenity statutes to suppress great works of art or literature. As Judge Augustus Hand said in *Ulysses* (72 F. 2d p. 708):

"* * * The foolish judgments of Lord Eldon about one hundred years ago, proscribing the works of Byron and Southey, and the

---

[25] It should be noted that if the book is obscene within § 1461 and thus barred from the mails it is a crime to ship it by express or in interstate commerce generally under 18 U. S. C. §§ 1462, 1465, and it would be subject to seizure by the customs authorities if imported for sale. (19 U. S. C. § 1305.)

finding by the jury under a charge by Lord Denman that the publication of Shelley's 'Queen Mab' was an indictable offense are a warning to all who have to determine the limits of the field within which authors may exercise themselves."

To exclude this book from the mails on the grounds of obscenity would fashion a rule which could be applied to a substantial portion of the classics of our literature. Such a rule would be inimical to a free society. To interpret the obscenity statute so as to bar "Lady Chatterley's Lover" from the mails would render the statute unconstitutional in its application, in violation of the guarantees of freedom of speech and the press contained in the First Amendment.

It may be, as the plaintiffs urge, that if a work is found to be of literary stature, and not "hard core" pornography, it is *a fortiori* within the protections of the First Amendment. But I do not reach that question here. For I find that "Lady Chatterley's Lover" is not obscene within the meaning of 18 U. S. C. § 1461, and is entitled to the protections guaranteed to freedoms of speech and press by the First Amendment. I therefore hold that the order of the Postmaster General is illegal and void and violates plaintiffs' rights in contravention of the Constitution.

Defendant's motion for summary judgment is denied. Plaintiff's cross-motions for summary judgment are granted. An order will issue permanently restraining the defendant from denying the mails to this book or to the circulars announcing its availability.

Settle order on notice.

Dated, New York, N. Y.
July 21, 1959

FREDERICK VANPELT BRYAN
U. S. D. J.